D1140698

HOW TO GIVE UP SMOKING

HOW TO GIVE UP SMOKING

LOULOU BROWN

CHANCELLOR
PRESS

First published in Great Britain in 1990 by Reed Consumer
Books Limited
as *Hamlyn Help Yourself Guide: How to Give Up Smoking*

This edition published in 1993 by Chancellor Press
an imprint of Reed Consumer Books Limited
Michelin House, 81 Fulham Road, London SW3 6RB
and Auckland, Melbourne, Singapore and Toronto

Reprinted 1994

Copyright © Reed International Books Limited 1990

All rights reserved. No part of this publication may be
reproduced, stored in a retrieval system, or transmitted,
in any form or by any means, electronic, mechanical,
photocopying, recording or otherwise, without the
permission of the publisher.

ISBN 1 85152 371 5

A CIP catalogue record for this book is available from
the British Library

Printed in Great Britain by Bath Press

Contents

Introduction

If you want to give up smoking but don't quite know how to go about it, this book is for you. It is also for the many smokers and non-smokers alike who think that something more has to be done to encourage those who smoke to stop, and to ensure that the very many young people who haven't smoked don't do so.

The way most people think about smoking has gradually changed a lot over the last thirty years. Smoking used to be thought of as fun and fashionable. It was very much the 'in thing' to do. Anyone who was interesting or, more to the point, who wanted to be seen to be interesting, smoked. It was also very much part of the business world. Cigarettes were smoked in most offices and it was considered friendly and polite to offer a cigarette to a stranger. A nervous person at an interview, for example, was thought to feel much better and more self-confident with a cigarette and would be pleased to be offered one by the interviewer.

Smoking seemed something very glamorous, exciting and sophisticated – remember Lauren Bacall, and the sultry Marlene Dietrich in the smoke-filled room in the *The Blue Angel*? In films, men who smoked seemed sexy, athletic and adventurous, while the women appeared to be both independent and feminine. Smoking lent a special quality to any scene. This is reflected in cigarette advertisements today where men are portrayed as macho cowboys and car mechanics, while women may be shown as somewhat forthright but still seductive and romantic.

The rich and famous smoked – and died. King George VI, Humphrey Bogart, Yul Bryner and Steve McQueen who all smoked heavily, died of lung cancer; it is almost certain they died because they smoked. It has now been established beyond all doubt that 90 per cent of all deaths from lung cancer are due to smoking.

Between 1962 and 1983, the Royal College of Physicians produced four reports which state very clearly that smoking is bad for the health. They estimate that every year 100,000 people in the UK die as a result of smoking, and write: '. . . it is almost unimaginable that at a time when major infectious diseases and malnutrition are potentially or actually conquerable mankind should inflict upon itself a totally unnecessary epidemic of smoking-related diseases.'

Smoking is no longer considered glamorous and romantic, rather, it is now seen as dirty, unpleasant, antisocial and dangerous, not only by those who don't smoke but very often by those who do. The present trend is towards giving up and creating a smoke-free atmosphere.

Unfortunately, giving up smoking is not something which is quick and simple that can be done instantly. Much the most effective method is the tortoise approach to giving up smoking. Slow and steady wins through in the end.

The reason why you smoke is all about how you think, the addiction to nicotine and many of the habits and associations which you pick up on the way while you're doing it. Once you have decided to give up, you have to make very careful plans before you have your last smoke. You have to think hard about what you believe to be true about smoking and you have to work out why you smoke. You also have to be quite sure that you really want to give up. For example, you might say you have to give up smoking, but before you do anything about it, you have to know that this is the right thing to do and really want to do it. You can do it, if you really want to, but you have to really want to before you can do it. All your thoughts must agree: stop smoking.

A lot of people say they can't give up. This is being very negative. What they probably mean is that they don't want to give up. Think positively instead. This means thinking about how strong and capable you really are, and how much better life is going to be without smoking.

Once you give up you have to deal not only with the withdrawal symptoms but also with the change in habits and life-style. You also have to make sure you never smoke again.

Although giving up smoking is hard work, without doubt it is the best thing to do. It most definitely *can* be done. Every day, lots of people give up; 11 million people in the UK have given up since the mid-1960s. Six out of ten people who still smoke say they would like to quit. That's about 8 million people in this country! Now, only one-third of all adults smoke, compared with nearly half in 1972.

It is your choice and for you to act. You may be persuaded by pressure from others who have already given up and from what you have heard, seen and read, and by the reasoned arguments put forward in this book, but it is still only you who can choose to give up and do it. No one can do the job for you. You have to choose, do the job and then stick by your decision and what you have done. It is up to you. YOU CAN DO IT!

Sprinkled throughout each chapter are a number of exercises and things to do. Please do what is suggested. Just reading the text won't be enough to ensure your commitment. There are a number of organizations mentioned throughout the book, all of which are listed, together with their addresses and telephone numbers on pp. 117–19.

ONE
━━━

The Dangers of Smoking

Smoking is about dependence, lack of choice and control, woolly mindedness and, above all, destruction. It is a sad story.

This chapter sets out the facts about smoking. The dangers have not been minimized and therefore do not make pleasant reading. Please, however, try to read through everything written. Take as long as you need, but do try to take in as much information as possible.

Well over 90 per cent of all tobacco products are hand-rolled, plain or filter cigarettes. About 3 per cent are cigars and cigarillos and the remaining 4 per cent smoked is pipe tobacco. Most of the time, therefore, it is cigarettes which are being referred to, unless other products are specifically mentioned.

The composition of tobacco

Tobacco contains many substances, the three most important of which are discussed below.

Nicotine, a colourless, oily compound, is the powerful drug responsible for smokers' dependence. The Royal College of Physicians has stated that: 'The most stable and well-adjusted person will, if he smokes at all, almost inevitably become dependent on the habit.' The college has also said that of teenagers who smoke more than a single cigarette, only 15 per cent avoid becoming regular dependent smokers.

Nicotine has an almost instant effect. A dose inhaled reaches the brain within seconds. It is distributed via the bloodstream to all parts of the body. If nicotine is not inhaled, which it usually isn't with smoking pipes and cigars, the drug is absorbed through the lining of the mouth to reach the bloodstream.

The effects of the drug are very wide ranging and to some extent paradoxical. For example, nicotine can both give you a lift or calm you down. The substance is very poisonous. If you swallow the nicotine from twenty cigarettes in one go, you will die. A very small amount, 0.002oz (about 60 mg) can kill an adult by paralysing the breathing.

Tar is formed by several thousand different compounds which are in the smoke when it is inhaled. Of the tar inhaled with every draw, up to 70 per cent is left in the airways and lungs. Tar contains sixty substances which have been shown to cause cancer when applied to living tissues.

Carbon monoxide is the same poisonous gas that exists within car exhaust fumes. The blood of a smoker may be carrying up to 15 per cent carbon monoxide instead of oxygen. This means, for example, that a cigarette smoker who lives at sea level is getting as little oxygen as a non-smoker at 8,000 ft (2,400 m).

Carbon monoxide is thought to be the major contributor to heart disease.

What goes wrong

Cilia The inhalation of tobacco smoke paralyses and sometimes destroys the tiny hairs, known as the cilia, which line the airways of the lungs. The cilia, with their constant beating, clean, filter and sterilize the air which is inhaled, but they cannot perform their function when damaged by the toxic action of hot tobacco smoke.

Smoker's cough Almost all heavy smokers, which the Royal College of Physicians defines as those who smoke twenty-five or more cigarettes a day, have a cough and some phlegm. This is usually only really bad in the morning, but it may persist all day.

The cough is produced by the cilia (see p. 11) which are trying to perform their function of removing toxic substances, particularly tar, from the lungs. The reason why the cough and phlegm are bad in the morning is that while the smoker is sleeping, he or she is not smoking. The cilia once more become active and start to remove the substances inhaled the day before. Ironically, a smoker's cough means the cilia are still effective.

Chronic bronchitis This is caused when there is an over-production of mucus, often as a result of the combination of nicotine, tar and carbon monoxide gas. There are increasing difficulties with breathing and often prolonged coughing and wheezing. Non-smokers very rarely get this disease.

Emphysema Severe chronic bronchitis may cause the very small, microscopic air spaces in the lungs, called alveoli, to burst, forming much larger air spaces. This means that the area within the lungs available for the exchange of gases, that is, the oxygen and carbon dioxide, is reduced and consequently more air has to be breathed to supply the oxygen the body needs. The result is emphysema, which causes breathlessness and an inability to move without tremendous exertion.

Arterial disease of the legs Nicotine may constrict the blood vessels which can lead to a hardening of the arteries of the legs.

Over 95 per cent of those who have arterial disease of the legs are smokers. The pain in the legs may be such that sufferers may not be able to walk 100 yd (90 m).

Cancers There are many different types of cancer caused by the tar formed by tobacco smoke.

Ninety per cent of all people with *lung cancer* have the disease as a result of smoking. Lung cancer kills nearly ten out of every hundred smokers in the UK – 30,000 people a year. The UK has the highest incidence of this disease in the world.

The risk increases directly in proportion to the number of cigarettes smoked. The younger the person is when starting to smoke, the greater the risk. If you stop smoking, the risks immediately stop increasing, and usually there is immediate improved lung function. With the majority of ex-smokers the lungs recover almost completely.

Other cancers known to be directly linked to smoking are: *cancers of the lip*, *cheek*, *tongue*, *larynx*, *oesophagus*, *pharynx*, *stomach*, *kidney*, *bladder*, *urinary tract*, and *pancreas*.

Peptic ulcers Eighty per cent of people who have peptic ulcers smoke. Nicotine increases the mobility of the bowel which speeds up the digestive process. This increases gastric acid secretion which can lead to an acid stomach and indigestion, which may precipitate the development of a peptic ulcer.

If you stop smoking, there is a 70 per cent chance of the ulcer healing without further treatment. If you continue to smoke, the ulcer will probably take a long while to heal.

Heart disease Coronary heart disease is the leading cause of death in the UK, and the numbers are rising. The disease is caused by both nicotine and carbon monoxide. Nicotine stimulates the production of adrenaline which increases the work of the heart by making it beat faster, causing the blood pressure to rise. The heart therefore needs more oxygen. However, the carbon monoxide binds to the haemoglobin in the blood so that the blood carries less oxygen. Both nicotine and carbon monoxide make it more likely that the blood will clot.

Angina When the heart muscle has to work hard, it needs more oxygen. When the blood carrying oxygen cannot pass through narrowed coronary vessels fast enough to deliver oxygen, the result is a pain in the chest known as angina.

Brain damage (stroke) Nicotine raises the hormone secretion from the adrenal gland. This raises the *blood pressure*. Nicotine also increases the heart rate and concentration of fatty acid in the smoker's blood. Fatty deposits reduce or block the blood supply in other parts of the body, leading to the possibility of brain damage.

Vision Tobacco smoke affects vision. Smokers are prone to allergic conjunctivitis, that is, watering and redness of the eyes. There is also an unpleasant eye disease directly related to smoking called tobacco ambylopia which results in partial loss of sight.

Other damage to the body Smoking may damage the upper parts of the digestive tract, including the mouth cavity, gums, teeth and tongue. Gingivitis, that is, inflammation of the gums and dental decay, are more common in smokers than in non-smokers.

Smoking has recently been linked with osteoporosis, that is, loss of calcium from the bones, which occurs particularly in women. It is also known to be linked with the following disorders: bad circulation, dizziness, excessive sweating, heart palpitations, hives (nettle rash), deafness, and periodic attacks of sinusitis and laryngitis.

Smoking and women

Smoking reduces oestrogen. It has been found that the more you smoke, the earlier you are likely to have the menopause.

Cancer of the cervix is more likely in women who smoke.

Women who smoke are more likely to be infertile, may take longer to conceive and have an increased risk of spontaneous abortion than women who do not smoke.

Smoking causes premature aging in women, particularly 'crow's feet' around the eyes.

Women who take the pill and smoke increase the risk of a heart attack and the risk increases with age. They are also more likely to have a stroke or blood clot in the legs. If you smoke twenty-five or more cigarettes a day and take the pill, you are forty times more likely to have a heart attack than a woman who neither smokes nor takes the pill.

Smoking and men

Smoking may result in low sperm count. It may also increase the risk of impotence. The link between smoking and damage to penile circulation is more than 90 per cent substantiated. Chronic impotence takes a long time to develop and most men associate it with growing old. Nevertheless, studies have shown that approximately 50 per cent of smokers who are impotent have erections again after stopping smoking for six or more weeks.

Fires and accidents

Smoking is thought to be the cause of about half the fires the fire brigade has to deal with. Nearly half of all household fires are the result of burning cigarettes, which are left unattended by smokers.

It is suggested that smoking can cause road accidents when smokers choke or light a cigarette, taking their eyes off the road momentarily.

Conclusion

The facts you've just read are not pleasant. Having now read and digested the information I hope you will agree that you have no choice but to give up smoking.

Chapter 2 makes much better reading and is full of life, optimism and hope. Before you start to read it, though, here are just a few statistics.

1 In the UK, one in every six deaths is caused by smoking.
2 If you smoke twenty-five cigarettes a day you have a one in eight chance of developing lung cancer.
3 Smoking causes seven times as many premature deaths as road accidents.
4 Of those who die prematurely because of smoking, heart disease claims 31 per cent; other diseases of the artery, including strokes 21 per cent; lung cancer 19 per cent; chronic bronchitis and emphysema 10 per cent; and the remaining 19 per cent are caused by other smoking related conditions.
5 As a direct result of smoking, 100,000 people in the UK die every year.
6 Smokers who smoke more than twenty cigarettes a day have twice as much time off work as non-smokers.
7 The cost to the National Health Service of treating smoking related diseases is over £170 million per year.

TWO

The Good Things About Giving Up

When you give up smoking, you are not only doing your body and mind good, you are also choosing to live rather than die. It's as simple as that. When you give up you will rediscover all sorts of pleasant things which have somehow disappeared while you have been smoking. For example, you will be able to taste things and look well and so much younger.

There are so many good things that will happen, almost immediately, that they will take a long time to list. You want to read about them? Surely you do! But perhaps you don't. Just as smokers don't want to know about the bad things which are happening to them, equally, they don't want to know about the good things, either. Why? Because in not knowing, it means they don't feel they have to stop. Remember: smoking is all about forgetting, fuzziness, not knowing.

Reading this chapter, the good news, is just as important as reading the bad news. Take as long as you like to read it. *But do read it*. Make sure you really concentrate.

The body
Your body will very quickly clean itself out and recover from the destruction you have caused. Remember, all the time it is

fighting a battle against tobacco. Once you start to let the body win, and treat it with respect, in almost all cases, it will triumph hands down. At once, you will start to build up more immunity to diseases. Not only will you be less likely to catch a cold or flu but, if and when you do catch something, it will clear up faster than before.

Remember, the risk of smoking is much more dependent on the length of time a person has smoked than on the amount smoked. Smoking two packets a day for twenty years is less dangerous than smoking one packet a day for forty years.

Things happen very quickly when you give up smoking. You will very soon look and feel like a completely different person, both inside and outside. Right now, I'm sure you are thinking, 'What rubbish!' So, to prove it isn't, we'll take a look at all parts of the body affected by tobacco, starting at the top and working downwards, and list the changes.

The hair will no longer be limp and smelly. It will regain its natural colour, no longer stained yellow by the smoke. When you give up it will become glossy and springy.

The head will clear. You may have had bad headaches as a result of the abundant mucus floating around the ears, nose and throat, caused by the phlegm. Once you stop, so do the headaches. If you suffer from migraines, there is no doubt that once you stop smoking these will lessen in number and severity. You won't feel dizzy in the morning from having lit your first cigarette of the day and inhaled the first dollop of nicotine for many hours. Your head and, indeed, your whole body won't have to wearily take on the daily battle against all those poisons which up until now you have insisted on pumping into yourself.

The eyes will no longer sting. When you smoke your eyes may be permanently red and watery, because they are allergic to cigarette smoke. When you give up, the watering, redness and stinging will stop and the eyes will be brighter and clearer. You will look younger, and others will notice you. If you wear contact lenses, you will be able to use them for much longer periods of time, and your sight may well improve.

The crow's feet wrinkles around the eyes which become prominent from years of smoking can be helped to fade by using skin creams. They will never disappear, but by stopping smoking you can slow down the aging of the skin quite considerably.

The nose won't be bunged up any more, also, it won't drip. You will start to smell things you haven't smelt in years. (Yes, I know there is a lot you don't want to smell, but think of all the good things.) Food, even the ordinary everyday items we eat, like bread, will give off a fantastic aroma! As for something like a lemon, which is sharp and rather acrid, it will hit you like a blast of fresh air by the seaside. Flowers, if you have a garden, will take you outside with all those new-found scents. Who knows, soon you might just be mowing the lawn – because you want to and not because you have to.

The ears will stop ringing. It may be that you suffer from partial deafness, because of all the mucus which has found its way into the middle ear. Almost as soon as you stop smoking, however, you will be able to hear better: the birds in the morning outside your bedroom window, a train, chugging away in the distance – and the cat miaowing to be let out. Your family won't have to bellow at you any more, and you can turn the television and radio down.

The lips will stop being chapped and dry.

The line around the lips, which develops from all the sucking on the cigarettes, once you have stopped smoking, can be helped to fade by the application of skin cream and daily massage.

The teeth will stay white after you have brushed them. There will be no more dirty, yellow stains.

The gums will change from a nasty browny-yellow colour to a healthy pink. They will remain firm and it is unlikely there will be very much more erosion.

The tongue will no longer be coated with a permanent yellow-white fur, and you will start to taste things again. For a short while after you stop smoking, say two weeks, part of your tongue may start to tingle faintly. Don't worry; it's just those taste-buds starting to work again. Everything will taste much sharper, so you won't need nearly so much salt or strong flavourings on your food. Just like a baby, you will discover all sorts of new, exciting tastes which have for a long while been dulled by smoking. Eating once again becomes a great pleasure.

The throat will stop being sore and you will lose that permanent huskiness, which may seem to you to be very sexy but is more likely to appear to others as though you are raddled.

The lungs will gradually turn pink and once more you will be able to breathe properly. Immediately you stop smoking, you reduce the risk of bronchitis, emphysema and lung cancer. The risk of lung cancer among people who have given up for ten years is less than half that of people who have continued to smoke. The risk of lung cancer for those who have not smoked for ten years but who probably smoked for twenty years is roughly the same as for life-long non-smokers.

You will gradually lose that shortness of breath and be able to walk longer distances. The hairs in the lungs, called the cilia (see p. 11) will start to work again. No longer flattened, they will be busy getting rid of all the gunge in the lungs. This means that for about two weeks after you stop smoking, you may be coughing more, not less, and bringing up even more of the muck you used to be bringing up every day in the morning. Don't worry, this is natural. The cilia and lungs as a whole are once more beginning to work as they should. They are getting rid of all the gunge created by the smoke inhaled into the lungs, especially the tar. (Do see your doctor if the cough continues for more than three weeks.)

The heart will begin to beat less frantically and those palpitations you might have been having every now and again will cease. Once you stop smoking, you immediately reduce the risk of heart disease. If you have had a heart attack, it is *never* too late to give up smoking. Survivors of a heart attack who continue to smoke are twice as likely to die of a second attack as those who give up.

The fingers won't have those familiar tobacco stains, caused by holding all those lighted cigarettes or cigars.

The feet won't feel so cold in winter. Many smokers suffer from poor circulation.

The skin will become a lot clearer and will stop looking lifeless. Your muscle tone will improve because you will be moving around a lot more.

ACTION

Once a day, whenever it suits you best, lie down on the floor and concentrate hard, with all your mind, on all parts of the body which are going to benefit when you stop smoking, starting at the top and working downwards. For one minute, think about your hair and then say to yourself: 'My hair is going to be much better when I stop smoking.' When you say this, really mean it. Now concentrate on your head and say: 'My head is going to be much better when I stop smoking.' Continue down the body.

The exercise should not take more than about twenty minutes.

Once you actually stop smoking, continue with this exercise for at least a month afterwards. Change the words slightly to: 'My hair is much better now that I've stopped smoking,' etc.

The mind

A great deal of the problem with giving up smoking is in the mind. Once you give up, you have done something very courageous and positive. You have given up a dependence and are now in control. To many smokers, this may sound mad. For them, smoking is about being in control: a drag on the cigarettes makes them feel all right, concentrated, able to cope with anything. Without tobacco, they fear the loss of control. In fact, all smoking is doing is satisfying the insidious craving for nicotine. *Smoking is about being dependent, being controlled.* When you give up you become much more in control of your life and gain freedom from addiction. You will feel you have power, because you have beaten the drug, and will feel much stronger emotionally.

Many of your worries will disappear when you give up. For example, you will lose the fear of contracting a disease related to smoking. You won't have to worry about offending others who don't smoke. You won't have to fuss about running out of tobacco after the shops have closed. No more wondering whether you can last out until the end of a meal at a dinner party.

About a month after you stop smoking, for the first time for many years you will be able to relax properly. Not only will your mind be easier because of the lack of worries, but you will be able to sleep much more soundly and wake up feeling refreshed after a good night's sleep. Far from relaxing, smoking actually speeds up the heart respiration rates and stimulates the production of adrenaline, so whenever you smoke, you are always being perked up, whether you like it or not.

Once you stop, you will feel far greater self-respect, not only for the way you are treating your body, but your whole self. You will have chosen a new life of self-awareness. In time, this will lead to consideration and caring not only for yourself but for others.

ACTION

As often as you can, think strong, positive thoughts about giving up smoking. Think how good your life is going to be, how much fitter you will be and how much more control you will have over what you do. Please do take this exercise seriously. It is no good being half-hearted about it. To win the battle against smoking means being single-minded and strong willed.

A popular person

With both body and mind in better shape you will become a different person. These days, giving up smoking means following the trend. You are going to be with the majority, and will no longer feel yourself to be an outcast or outsider. Without quite realizing why, you will be making new friends. People who have previously shunned you will want to know you. Suddenly the world is a friendlier place: you have become popular.

Smoking can act as a barrier against close contact with other people – unless they are smokers. Those who don't smoke hate the smell of tobacco smoke; the way smokers wheeze and constantly clear their throats; the way they often have to blow their noses, even though they have no colds; the way they always leave a mess behind them of ash-trays full of stale butt ends; the way they won't walk anywhere but always have to travel in the car, bus or underground, even if the journey is only a street or two away . . . the list of these dreary nuisances seems to be endless.

When you give up, you won't smell – or if you do, you'll smell nice and fresh. You won't wheeze, you won't clear your throat, you won't blow your nose, you won't leave ash-trays full of cigarette ends. Now you will be able to go with non-smokers on walks, instead of driving everywhere. Your hair will be glossy, your eyes will sparkle, you will be full of energy – and the best thing of all is that you will look years younger.

If you are the only one who smokes in your family, you will be even happier than most people who give up. When you give up you will be welcomed back into the fold like a prodigal son or daughter after a very long time away from the home. Your non-smoking family who have waited for years for this to happen, will be overjoyed. Everyone will want to help and encourage you. You will be fussed over and treated like royalty, even though secretly you may think you don't deserve this treatment. May be, if you think about it, you do. You will have taken a tremendous step in the right direction and deserve all praise.

At work, too, life will suddenly change for the better. You won't have to work separately from the majority of your colleagues any more. If you work with people who smoke, when you stop, ask to be transferred to a non-smoking office immediately. If you boss does not agree to this, he is not worth working for. In this case, go to someone higher up the ladder in the organization. Be brave and demand your rights. Remember that, as a non-smoker working in an office with smokers, your right to work in a healthy atmosphere is being eroded.

Suddenly, too, when you give up you will find much more time to do things, which will probably be a blessed relief. All those things in the 'In' tray which haven't been attended to can now be dealt with. Now you don't have to stop working, scrabble around for the packet of cigarettes and matches, light up and then search for an ash-tray which you've somehow mislaid. There is now no break for all those cigarettes. You will work methodically and achieve more.

'Ah!', I can hear you saying, 'But I won't be able to concentrate any longer.' That is nonsense. It is true that the nicotine quickly speeds up the heart rate and triggers the release of adrenaline, but there is no way that it can be said that you concentrate better by smoking than by doing without. For the first three weeks after you give up smoking you will find it difficult to concentrate because you will be suffering withdrawal symptoms from the lack of nicotine. You will feel an insistent nagging at the back of your mind, a feeling of emptiness, of something being not quite right, of restlessness. After this time, however, you will almost certainly no longer feel the cravings and in almost all cases the addiction to nicotine will have ceased. You will be able to concentrate better than when you smoked, because you won't have to keep on stopping what you are doing every half hour or so. You will be able to work for far longer periods at a time. You will be less easily distracted.

Saving money

Have you ever counted up the cost of smoking? You may know the exact cost of a packet of cigarettes and may even know how much you spend a week on tobacco. Did you know that if you smoke a packet a day you are spending about £600 a year? Think of what you could do with all that money. It will not only cover your 'poll tax' but probably give you something to spend on a big treat for yourself. If you think of what you will be saving over a 50-year period, the mind boggles. The amount is simply staggering! It is about £30,000, enough to buy yourself a big car, go on a cruise round the world, have wall-to-wall carpets in every room in the house, and also have a brand new kitchen with all the latest gadgetry.

What about the other, more hidden, expenses? For example, life insurance premiums and endowment mortgages are less expensive for a non-smoker. Your rooms will be much cleaner. You don't, of course, have to pay for your office cleaning bills, but what about the costs of cleaning the rooms at home? Think of all the money you will be saving on carpet, curtain and upholstery cleaning, as well as on dry-cleaning bills. Quite apart from all the energy you will save from less cleaning! Nor will you have to spend so much money on shampoo, perfume, mouth-washes or breathmints, just to smell nice.

ACTION

Think of something really big you want to spend money on. How about that holiday in Australia where your sister lives? Find out the cost. Then, once you have stopped smoking, start to put aside the money you spent on cigarettes for the holiday – or whatever takes your fancy. The exhilaration of being able to travel to new places, buy special items you never thought would be affordable, and even splash out on a completely impractical pair of shoes will more than make up for any feelings of loss. More than likely you won't feel any loss but be marvelling at the extra money in your pocket.

You know, more or less, how many packets you smoked in

a week, so at the beginning of each new week, or month, if that's easier, put the money saved into a special savings account. You will be amazed at how fast it builds up, and you'll be able to afford that extra special grand treat sooner than you think.

THREE

Why Do You Smoke?

If you want to give up smoking, you have to find out why you smoke. Once you have worked out why you smoke, you can then learn to stop smoking. You cannot become committed to stopping smoking until you understand the very many resistances you have to changing your lifestyle. Once you know about and understand the pressures you are under to continue smoking, you can start to do something about them.

Finding out why you smoke is not as easy as it sounds, because to do the job properly means you have to separate out your attitudes towards smoking from the reasons why you smoke. You also have to remember why you started to smoke.

This chapter is very long because it sets out three different stages in learning about why you smoke. Please take as much time as you need to read it and do the exercises listed. They are very important in helping you to reach a commitment to quit. Remember: slow and steady wins through in the end!

Smokers' attitudes to smoking appear to vary a great deal. There are some who really do think that what they do is harmful not only to themselves but to others as well. They would, they think, love to give up but fatalistically accept that they are 'hooked' on the 'habit' for life.

There are others, much more vociferous, who claim that they are fine, thank you very much, and just want to be left alone to enjoy their 'freedom' to smoke. They don't want to be badgered by sanctimonious do-gooder nuisances.

The vast majority of smokers try hard not to think about what they do. This, however, is becoming much more difficult, partly a result of pressure from non-smokers and the ever-increasing number of ex-smokers. It is also because the evidence that smoking damages the health is now irrefutable, and that there are now many more no-smoking areas than there were even, say, five years ago. Smokers are having to revert to ghetto-like tactics, smoking in corners at parties and often being forced to associate with each other, whether they really like to or not.

Smokers' attitudes towards smoking

Smokers' attitudes have two main features in common. They tend to be both vague and inaccurate. This is because woolly-mindedness suits them. If they had to think properly, they wouldn't like the thoughts that came up. They wouldn't like what they had to do, either. The only action possible after reading the available evidence, set out in chapters 1 and 2, is to give up smoking. Smokers, however, prefer to sit on the fence and mouth vague platitudes. It is much easier to do this; that way you don't have to be committed to anything – nor do you have to take any decisive action.

Below are some examples of what smokers say about smoking followed by some reasoned arguments to help clear up thinking on the subject. Please read these carefully.

1 **'I'm much too young for smoking to affect me; I'll give up when I'm older.'**
[Reply] What do you mean young? Exactly how old are

you? Remember: anyone at any age is affected by smoking. It is potentially dangerous for everyone, no matter how young.

If you really are young and have not been smoking for long, bear in mind that you will probably find it more difficult to give up later because you will become dependent on the nicotine and will have formed habits which will be hard to break. Don't wait. GIVE UP NOW.

2 **'I'm all right. Don't you worry about me! I'll stop if I get anything.'**
[Reply] How do you know if you are all right? Have you been to your doctor recently? Smokers under the age of forty-five visit their doctors 40 per cent more often than non-smokers, and in-patient demand on hospital services is 71 per cent more than for non-smokers.

Have you thought that you might die if you 'get anything'? Ninety-three per cent of those diagnosed as having lung cancer die within five years.

3 **'I'm OK. I only smoke a few.'**
[Reply] What do you call 'a few'? Five, ten, fifteen, twenty a day? The Royal College of Physicians defines a heavy smoker as one who smokes more than twenty-five cigarettes a day. How many do you smoke a day? Have you any idea?

Please remember that *there is no safe level of consumption*. About one-third of all premature deaths caused by smoking occur in smokers who smoke fewer than twenty cigarettes a day. The chances are that you are one of the 98 per cent of smokers who are 'proper' smokers; there are only 2 per cent of smokers who only smoke occasionally.

If you really are an occasional smoker, please don't ever smoke again.

4 **'All these goddam statistics! They are only mumbo-jumbo. There is no real evidence to connect smoking with ill-health.'**
[Reply] Statistics are the opposite of mumbo-jumbo and there is now a wealth of evidence linking smoking with a number of diseases (see chapter 1, p. 12). Please don't run away while I list some statistics for you. They are quite easy to understand – if you let yourself understand them.

One in four (one quarter) of all heavy smokers will die of a disease linked to smoking. A 'heavy smoker', remember, according to the Royal College of Physicians, is one who smokes more than twenty-five cigarettes a day.

Over 90 per cent of all deaths from lung cancer are caused by smoking. In 1920 in Britain there were 250 recorded deaths from lung cancer. By 1960, this figure had risen to 10,000. Now, in 1990, the figure is 40,000. Ninety per cent of 40,000 is 36,000. Don't you think these figures show something?

5 **'I smoke cigars; they are healthier than cigarettes.'**
[Reply] They are not. If you inhale cigar smoke you will be doing your lungs more damage more quickly than if you smoked cigarettes. The tar levels in cigars are very high. Even if you don't inhale there is still a strong likelihood they will do damage to your health. It is simply not worth the risk.

Remember: *all* tobacco products are potentially lethal. There are *none* that are safe.

31

6 'Smoking cannot be all that dangerous, otherwise the government would have done something about it.'

[Reply] You seem to have a very high opinion of the government, as though all its members knew exactly what was good or bad, right or wrong. In fact this is not so, and the government's approach to smoking has been very inconsistent, mainly because its members disagree on policy to be adopted (see chapter 10, p. 112).

Why don't you do some learning and thinking for yourself? Read around for facts; make you own judgements. Don't rely on anyone else to make up your mind for you.

7 'I smoke because I enjoy it.'

[Reply] What do you enjoy? The taste? The smell? The mess? The cravings? The habit? The associations? The worries? Please think very hard indeed about what it is exactly that you do enjoy. What form of pleasure is it that you get?

It may be that you do, genuinely, enjoy something about smoking. If you want to give up you are going to have to work especially hard, to make sure that you know that the disadvantages of smoking far outweigh the advantages.

You may well find that, in thinking about it, what you previously thought you enjoyed in fact you really find a boring but necessary process to go through at regular intervals. The 'pleasure' is really the relief at obtaining the nicotine you require to relieve the craving caused by withdrawal from the nicotine. That is no pleasure; that is a vicious circle; it is dependence.

8   **'I'll be all right, because even if I do get something, modern medicine and surgical techniques will be able to put it right.'**
[Reply] There are no miracle cures. Please remember that every year 100,000 people die of diseases related to smoking.

Are you really prepared to put your health and possibly life at risk just to smoke? Doesn't this seem a rather drastic thing to do? How about the people closest to you, have you thought of them?

9   **'I can't live without smoking.'**
[Reply] Why not? Have you ever tried to give up? Even though you are probably dependent on nicotine and have formed quite strong habits and associations with smoking, there are very many good reasons for giving up, and you most certainly can give up.

You were not born to smoke and there are no reasons for thinking that the dependence and habits are forever fixed and cannot be changed. Remember: no one ever died from giving up smoking.

10   **'All my friends are smokers; I can't do without my friends.'**
[Reply] Very probably the people with whom you associate are indeed smokers, who tend to congregate together in a world which is increasingly set against them. Think: are the people with whom you associate really your friends? Don't you think you are with these people because you smoke rather than because you have anything else in common?

Even if they really are your friends, why do you think you will have to do without them if you don't smoke?

Surely the bond of friendship is stronger than the bond of smoking for companionship? If you give up, you can encourage your friends to give up, too. Doesn't that make sense?

ACTION

Having read the above ten smokers' statements and the responses to them, make up five of your own – or more if you like. You have your own attitudes to smoking, which may be very different to the ones recorded above. The one rule is that for every quote there must be a reasoned response.

If at present you don't know how to argue with a smoker's statement, first read this book through from beginning to end and then read some others. Ask for some books on giving up smoking at your local library. Once you have read a bit and have some knowledge to back up your arguments you will find it a lot easier. Remember, though, that you may well be arguing against yourself. This is both difficult and painful, but absolutely necessary if you want to become committed to giving up smoking.

Why did you start to smoke?

Once upon a time you smoked a pipe for the first time or lit up your first cigar or cigarette – and this was almost certainly not a pleasant experience. Probably you spluttered, choked and felt rather sick. To begin with, you almost certainly didn't inhale, but blew clouds of smoke around yourself, pretending that this was grand. Secretly, you may have felt rather worried about not knowing what to do and disliked doing something which made you feel nasty and look rather silly. But the pressures on you to smoke were very strong . . .

Below are given ten reasons for why you might have started

smoking. It is assumed you started to smoke under the age of twenty-one, as if you reach that age and have never smoked you will very probably never do so. If, however, you started to smoke when in your twenties or even later, it is still useful to read this section, even though it will not be directly relevant.

1   'Smokers seemed mature, tough and sophisticated. They were grown up, so I followed their example.'

2   'Smoking was forbidden, so it was exciting. I was a rebel, so it followed that I smoked.'

3   'All my friends smoked. I would have been left out if I hadn't smoked. I wouldn't have been one of the gang.'

4   'There was all this stuff about smoking. I was dead curious to know what it was all about, first hand experience, and all that.'

5   'Smoking made you feel as though you were somebody; those who didn't smoke were nobodies.'

6   'My parents and brothers and sisters smoked. There were fags left all over the place at home. It seemed natural to follow the rest.'

7   'I was no good at anything when I was a kid. I was always bottom in class at school; I had terrible greasy skin and spots; and I was really shy. Smoking gave me confidence. I felt I was in control.'

8   'I wanted to keep thin, because otherwise my boyfriend would have left me. Smoking was the only way to do it, because that way I didn't feel hungry and didn't eat so much.'

9   'I got so bored when I was a teenager. There was never anything I really liked doing. Smoking gave me something to do. It was a ritual lighting up, finding the right time, the

35

right place, the right gear.'

10 'I wasn't much good at anything at school, except art. We had this teacher who was great, and who chain-smoked. We all tried to copy him and learnt to smoke.'

Think hard about these ten reasons for starting to smoke. They don't seem to add up to much do they? Only one, number 4, seems even remotely positive. The rest are about conforming (numbers 1, 3, 6, 8 and 10), or smoking providing a crutch to lean on (numbers 5 and 7) or bucking the system (numbers 2 and 9). They don't seem to be very good reasons for starting along the road of dependence and ill-health.

ACTION

If you are still young and have not been smoking for very long, don't waste any more time. *Stop now!* You will almost certainly find it easier than people older than you, because you are probably not yet addicted to the nicotine and have not yet formed strong habits or associations. Even if you don't want to stop, please read the rest of the book, in fairness to yourself and others.

If you have been smoking for some time, perhaps one or more of the quotations listed above seem more or less to fit the reasons why you started. If this is so, spend at least ten minutes each day for the next week thinking about these reasons. Write down what you felt at the time. When you started to smoke, did you feel good? Did you feel you were joining in? Were you following the leader? Was the smoke pleasant? Did it make you feel sick? Be honest and really work hard at this.

Quite possibly, none of the reasons given above for starting to smoke seem to fit your own experience. If so, think hard about why you started. Write down the reasons as they really were – everything about them – and think about them for ten minutes each day for the next week.

At the end of this seven-day period, you should know a lot about your reasons for starting to smoke. You are now ready to consider the reasons why you smoke.

Why do you smoke?

Below are listed ten reasons why you might smoke. There are also some responses to these reasons given below each quotation. The reasons given for smoking now are not very dissimilar to the attitudes smokers have about smoking or the reasons given for why smokers first started to smoke. They are, however, somewhat clearer and more honest.

By this time you will probably have done a lot of thinking about the reasons for smoking and are yourself clearer in your mind and more honest about the reasons for smoking than you were when you began to read this chapter.

1 **'I have to have a fix, at fairly regular intervals. Otherwise I get pangs. After a while I get restless and cannot concentrate properly.'**
[Reply] It sounds as if you are a heavy smoker. These pangs are withdrawal symptoms, one of the unpleasant side effects of smoking. Most heavy smokers experience withdrawal symptoms after about half an hour or so without a cigarette. The nicotine level in the bloodstream is depleted very rapidly and cravings are experienced in the form of restlessness and lack of concentration and sometimes a feeling of emptiness.

Nicotine is a very powerful drug, and heavy smokers can function normally only with a high level of nicotine in the bloodstream – which, of course, can only be maintained by constant smoking. This tops up the nicotine to the required level.

One thing, though. Have you ever thought about why it is you can get through most of the night without smoking? You don't smoke when you're asleep. So the withdrawal symptoms can't be that bad. You really can stop smoking, even if the cravings are bad.

2   **'I realize now that I've never really thought about smoking. It's always just been part of my life, like brushing my teeth, or talking, or eating.'**
[Reply] That is a really good, honest admission. You are well on the way to a strong commitment to quitting. However, you should think a lot about smoking now. You may be a heavy smoker for whom smoking is an automatic process. Perhaps you light up without thinking, and for much of the time are unaware of this. Maybe you are also unaware of how many times a year you go to the doctor or for what reasons. Perhaps you don't know how unpleasant your smoking is for others who live or work with you, or what harm you are doing to yourself and them.

If you are such a smoker, begin right away to keep a diary of every cigarette you have each day. Note the time of day, the number of times you light up and note why you lit up when you did. That way you will start to be able to focus properly on your smoking.

3   **'I can't relax without a fag.'**
[Reply] This probably means you are restless and fidgety because you are experiencing a craving for a smoke. Once

you've got some more nicotine inside you, you will be 'OK' because you'll be topped up.

In fact you don't really relax because nicotine speeds up the heart respiratory rates and stimulates the production of adrenaline.

4 'I need to concentrate; I need a lift.'
[Reply] Again, this probably means you are restless and fidgety because you are experiencing a craving for a smoke. Once you've got your fix you will be boosted up. You will be able to concentrate and think better. You won't seem so tired and you will be able to withstand monotonous tasks. Well done, nicotine.

5 'I smoke to take my mind off things. I've got so many worries these days. I smoke to cope.'
[Reply] Smoking tends to blur proper thinking, so perhaps it does take your mind off things. Maybe, too, you smoke to make yourself feel more self-confident, like you did when you were younger.

If you stopped smoking you would actually have fewer worries. You wouldn't be anxious about diseases related to smoking, or how your smoking is affecting other people, or what other people think about you smoking. That's quite a lot you wouldn't have to think about any more.

6 'I have to have something to fiddle with, and I don't seem to be able to go a long time without a cigarette in the mouth.'
[Reply] It would seem you use smoking to fulfil very strong oral and manipulatory needs. Perhaps, too, you are fond

of the paraphernalia of smoking: the cigarettes, ash-trays, lighters, filters, as well as the ritual of lighting up.

Think, though, of how much more time you will save and how much freer you will be without the incessant fiddling, the constant drawing on the cigarette, the coughing, the wheezing, the smoke . . . You *can* change your habits and stop the dependence.

7   **'There are certain times of the day when I have to have a fag. For example, there's the fag after breakfast, the fag first thing when I get to the office, the fag with my coffee break . . .'**
[Reply] Smoking fairly rapidly becomes a matter of habit; there are associations formed with it. These are quite apart from the cravings experienced. So that it becomes a habit to have a cigarette with a cup of tea or coffee – *any* cup of tea or coffee. At the same time, coffee or tea become associated with a smoke.

There are a lot of knots to untangle. Smoking is not only about dependence on nicotine. To stop smoking means one has to work hard to break the habits (chapter 8, see p. 86) and associations (chapter 9, see p. 95). They can be broken and your life can change. Don't despair. You *can* do without.

8   **'I smoke to keep slim. I would be overweight otherwise.'**
[Reply] Is keeping thin really more important to you than your health or the effect your habit is having on other people? It would seem your priorities are a bit askew, to say the least. Who are you really trying to please, yourself or other people, and why?

Anyway, perhaps you haven't noticed, but there are plenty of fat smokers, some of whom are most definitely overweight. Smoking is not the answer to weight control. Although it is true that you may gain some weight when you stop smoking (because you might eat more and your metabolic rate is almost certain to change), you probably won't put on very much. With careful attention to your diet, you will lose this weight gain fairly rapidly. Please note that there are many people who have given up smoking who have not put on any weight at all. You never know, you might be one of them.

9 **'I just need time to be by myself occasionally, and then I have to have a cigaratte. It is a great comfort.'**
[Reply] It sounds as though you might be a woman with far too many demands on your life and time. Perhaps you are a wife and mother, working woman and housewife, cook and cleaner, childminder and secretary . . . or alternatively a stressed-out executive with constant demands on your time from early in the morning until late at night.

Of course you want time to yourself. It is a treat. Is smoking also a treat? Is there really nothing else you could give yourself in your precious free time?

Smoking is not just anti-social; it can kill, you know.

10 **'I smoke for pleasure – to make things which are good even better. Like after sex, for instance . . .'**
[Reply] Sex is even better if you don't smoke (see chapter 1, p. 15).

It is possible, though not yet proven, that smoking is a

pleasurable activity. It has recently been suggested that nicotine acts on the pleasure centre of the brain. Once activated you very quickly learn to ask for more, but it is a deadly pleasure. If this is the case you must un-learn what has been learned. There will be many more real pleasures once you have given up smoking.

ACTION

Now that you've read through these ten reasons for smoking, please think very carefully. Do one or more of them relate to the reasons you smoke in any way? If they do, think about the responses to the quotations, are they justified? If not, write down why not. Argue with the quotations, the responses – and with yourself.

If none of the quotations seem relevant to you, think hard and write down why you smoke now. When you have written down why, argue with yourself. *Don't* make excuses and be as honest as you can. You are learning to think clearly and to face facts. It is a difficult and painful process, and means you have to change the way you think. You can do this if you are determined. If you are really determined it will seem an easy exercise.

Having read through this chapter and done all the exercises, you should now be ready to move on to chapter 4.

FOUR

Stopping Smoking

This chapter is about how to make the decision to give up smoking. It is the most important chapter in the book, because once you have *really* made the decision to quit, the doing, the actual quitting and change in your lifestyle that follows should be easy.

The introduction and first three chapters were to do with learning about smoking: the dangers to health, the good things which will happen when you give up and the reasons why you smoke.

You now know quite a lot about yourself and smoking. You know that when you first smoked you didn't like anything at all about what you were doing: the taste, the smell, feeling sick . . ., but you persevered and now you don't notice these things.

The truth about smoking

What is smoking doing to you? Be really honest and think very hard. Do you have one or more of the following problems?

1 **When you wake up in the morning, do you cough a great deal and bring up a lot of phlegm?**
   If yes, you are probably a heavy smoker (twenty-five or more cigarettes a day, remember). During the night while you've been sleeping, the cilia have been working –

because you haven't been smoking – to remove the tar and mucus from the lungs.

2 Do you wheeze a lot?
If yes, this means the smoking is having an effect on your lungs, making it difficult for you to breathe.

3 Do you find it difficult to run fast and for a long time?
If yes, this may well mean you have been smoking for some time and find it difficult to breathe fast and deep because your lungs are clogged up.

4 Do you think that people who don't smoke tend to avoid you?
If yes, you are almost certainly correct. They avoid you because you smell unpleasant to them, and, perhaps, because they can't abide the smoke or your coughing and wheezing . . .

5 Do you find your burn holes in your clothes, carpets and furniture?
If yes, this is because smoking is about fire and burning. Bits of burning tobacco are often inadvertently flicked around, causing damage.

6 Do you get agitated because you often run out of cigarettes or cigars in the middle of a long meeting at the office, or late at night when the shops are closed, or first thing in the morning before they are open?
If yes, you are probably dependent on nicotine which makes you want to smoke very badly and sometimes seems to nearly drive you mad.

7   Do you feel intimidated by people in the office or people you meet at parties who don't smoke?
If yes, this is probably because the trend is for people not to smoke. You are in the minority and may feel a bit persecuted.

8   Since you started to smoke, have you been getting lots of colds and coughs which always take a long time to clear up?
If yes, this is because smoking has a damaging effect on the cilia, which cannot perform their protective function on the lungs when damaged by toxic tobacco smoke. Illnesses will take much longer to clear up because your body has been affected by the poisons you have been inhaling. Your body is constantly battling against diseases which you are inflicting on yourself, and has less resistance.

9   Do other people criticize you for needing so much salt and pepper and hot sauces on your food, and do you find most things you eat rather boring these days?
If yes, this is because your senses of smell and taste have been deadened by smoking.

10   Do you find that you can't afford to smoke?
The answer to this should be a resounding yes. You cannot afford to smoke, not only because tobacco products are expensive to buy but also because you are putting your health at risk.
ACTION
Almost certainly, you suffer at least one and probably several effects of smoking listed above. Are there any more you can think of?

1 Take a large piece of paper and pen or pencil and draw a line down the middle. Head the left-hand column 'The bad things that smoking does to me' and the right-hand column 'What will happen when I stop?' Draw a line across both columns, underneath the headings.

   In the left-hand column, make a note of every bad effect you can think of that smoking has on you. Number each effect. Under each effect, draw a line, so that it is separated out from all the other effects. Take as long as you need to write this list. Make sure this list contains every single effect you can think of. If you need to, continue the chart onto a second, or even third piece of paper.

2 When you have finished, read through what you have written and think hard about it. Nothing you have listed will make very pleasant reading. It doesn't bear thinking about, really, does it? That's the point. You have to think about these things to achieve your commitment to quit. Writing them down forces you to take the information in. However much you are tempted to stop writing, or call a halt to the list, resist it and keep writing.

3 Now for something more pleasant. In the right-hand column, side by side with each effect of smoking, list what will happen when you stop smoking. Again, under each item, draw a line. If you have read chapter 2 (p. 17), you will know a lot of the things that will happen when you stop smoking, so if you haven't already done so, read it now. If the answer isn't there, phone ASH or QUIT for advice (see pp. 117–19).

   By the time you have finished, your chart should look something like the following – only much longer. Try to aim for two or three pages.

THE BAD THINGS THAT SMOKING DOES TO ME	WHAT WILL HAPPEN WHEN I STOP?
a I cough and bring up phlegm.	I'll bounce out of bed in the morning and be bright and breezy.
b I wheeze.	I will be able to breathe easily.
c I can't run.	I'll be able to run again.
d People avoid me.	People will want to be with me.
e I burn holes in my clothes, carpets and furniture.	My clothes, carpets and furniture will stay clean and safe from fire.
f I get agitated when I run out of cigars and cigarettes and can't get hold of any.	I will be calm and free of dependence.
g I am afraid of people who don't smoke.	I will be glad to be with people who don't smoke because I'll be one of them.
h I get endless coughs and colds.	I'll get fewer coughs and colds.

THE BAD THINGS THAT SMOKING DOES TO ME	WHAT WILL HAPPEN WHEN I STOP?
i I can't taste or smell.	I'll be able to taste and smell much more.
j Smoking uses up my money.	I'll have more money when I stop.

It shouldn't need saying that everything in the right-hand column is a plus. EVERYTHING ABOUT GIVING UP SMOKING IS POSITIVE. There is nothing bad at all.

4 For a week after you have made this list, please spend ten minutes each day reading through what you have written, both in the left-hand and right-hand columns, and thinking very hard about your attitudes and feelings. Do you care? Do you think smoking is dangerous? Do you think it is all a load of rubbish? Do you feel upset? Do you feel angry? Add as many things as you can think of to the list. At the end of the week, think about what you might do in the future. Do you think you are now near to making the decision to quit?

5 Now make another list. This time, it is all the good things you can think of about smoking. By now, with all the learning and thinking and exercises you've been doing, you should be able to list the bad things without any difficulty. Can you think of any 'good things' you will miss when you give up smoking? To help you, there are a few below.

   (a) Smoking is a real pleasure; I will be sad to lose this pleasure.

   (b)   I will be sad not to be able to mix with my smoking friends.

   (c)   I'll lose the control I had over my weight.

   (d)   I'll lose the ability to be sociable if I don't smoke.

   (e)   I'll lose a support when in need.

6 Make yet another list with a line down the middle. Head the two columns 'Things I shall miss when I give up', and 'Why I won't really miss them'. In the left-hand column, write down everything you can think of that you will miss. Take your time. Don't leave out anything. In the right-hand column, list the arguments against the things you will miss. Number each item and draw a line under each entry when you have finished. For instance:

THINGS I SHALL MISS WHEN I GIVE UP	WHY I WON'T REALLY MISS THEM
a Smoking is a real pleasure.	Yes, but it's a deadly pleasure. I'll feel better when I give up and find other pleasures in life.
b I will be sad not to mix with my smoking friends.	I will still mix with them and will encourage them not to smoke.
c I'll lose the control I had over my weight.	I never did have control over my weight. Even if I do put on some after I stop, I should be able to lose it.

THINGS I SHALL MISS WHEN I GIVE UP	WHY I WON'T REALLY MISS THEM
d I'll lose the ability to be sociable if I don't smoke.	I'll really be much more sociable if I don't smoke. I'll meet many more people who will want to know me.
e I'll lose a support when in need.	I need a poisonous prop such as smoking like a hole in the head! Smoking is no real support.

By the time you have finished this list, you should have argued against everything you can think of that seemed good about smoking. There should be nothing left to *really* make you want to smoke. By now, you should be very near to a commitment to quitting.

A strong-willed, single-minded commitment

In chapter 2 you were given exercises to do for helping the body and mind. You should still be doing these every day. Are you? If not, please read or re-read chapter 2 (pp. 17–27) again and start to do them. Please try to do these exercises for at least a month before you give up.

Sitting on the fence You need to become single-minded in your commitment. That means having one thought only about giving up. That thought should be 'I'm going to give up'. It should not be: 'I'll give up sometime but not just now, thank you. It's a big decision and I can't think straight, right now.' Or:

'Yes, smoking is bad for me, but giving up is quite impossible. I've got enough to cope with as it is.' Or: 'One day I'll certainly give up but right now there's such a lot on my mind, I can't concentrate on anything much at the moment – life is such a rush.'

It is sometimes very hard to make a decision, even about matters which seem fairly straightforward. For example, you've agreed to go out to the cinema with your best friend. You know you will be relaxed and will have a good time. But then someone whom you've only recently met, and rather fancy, wants to meet you for a meal on the same evening.

You have to make a choice. Part of your mind says one thing and part the other. Which will win? Perhaps the agony is too much and instead you decide to go out for a drink with someone completely different simply to appease the battling factions in your mind.

With giving up smoking, however, it's different. You can no longer sit on the fence and you can't be in two or more minds. You must get off that fence and be of one mind.

There is only one choice: to give up. You can continue to live in the same way as before or choose to change. You cannot choose to continue smoking, because you have no choice. You are dependent on the nicotine and by force of habit and association continue to smoke. You can choose to be independent, but you cannot choose to be dependent, just as you can choose to break the habit but cannot choose the habit.

To give up smoking means you have to choose.

It's *your* choice Some people seem to find it quite easy to make decisions; others dither in messy uncertainties for ages, or have their minds made up by others who can't stand their indecisiveness any longer. If you are going to give up smoking, it is very important that *you* make the decision to give up and that every part of your mind is in agreement with this. Don't let yourself be bullied by others. Make your own judgements. Only by making up your own mind, rather than having it made up for you, can you become certain about what you want to do and be single-minded in your objective.

Remember what was said in the introduction: you have to think hard about what you believe to be true about smoking and to work out why you smoke. You also have to be quite sure that you really want to give up. You have to know that this is the right thing to do and really want to do it. *REMEMBER:* YOU CAN DO IT, IF YOU REALLY WANT TO, BUT YOU HAVE TO REALLY WANT TO DO IT BEFORE YOU CAN DO IT.

You need a lot of will power to stop smoking. Will power is only achieved by being single-minded. Single-mindedness is only achieved by making your own judgements, and you can only make your own judgements by thinking for yourself and not relying on others to do your thinking for you.

This may sound very complicated. Let's put it another way. Thinking for yourself means you can make your own judgements and become single-minded, which will give you will power. So:

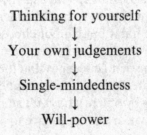

Thinking for yourself
↓
Your own judgements
↓
Single-mindedness
↓
Will-power

Decision time

You have learned about smoking and about yourself, and you have thought long and hard. It's time to make the decision to stop smoking. If you don't yet feel ready to do so, re-read the introduction and the first four chapters of this book, including this one, and continue to do the exercises. Otherwise make the decision to give up. Now!

FIVE

How to Stop Smoking

Giving up smoking is all about knowing, doing and changing. Before you give up, you need to know about the dangers of smoking (chapter 1, p. 10) and the good things which will happen when you give up (chapter 2, p. 17). You also, and this is particularly important, have to know why you smoke (chapter 3, p. 28). Above all else, you must know that you can give up (chapter 4, p. 43). So the introduction and the first four chapters of this book are about the knowing. This chapter is about doing and changing.

If you haven't already done so, read the introduction and chapters 1 to 4 now. Try to concentrate as hard as you can. You may find this difficult as much of the information is unpleasant to read. Even the good news may not seem so pleasant, unless you are absolutely sure that you do want to give up. Please do the exercises set out in each chapter. There are no excuses for not doing them; giving up smoking is most definitely not about excuses.

Even if you have read the chapters already, it is a good idea to read them again, now, just to make sure that you have all the knowledge you need and are now single-minded enough to give up.

Before setting out what to do when you give up, it is important to know what you should not do.

The Mark Twain method of giving up smoking

There are a great many smokers who one day, for no particular reason, say to themselves something like this: 'I've had enough of smoking. I've just been promoted; the sun is shining; life is good; I'll give up now.' They then, like Mark Twain, try not to smoke and are astonished to find that only the next day, again like Mark Twain, they have 'borrowed' at least one cigarette from a smoking colleague. ('Borrowing' is smokers' talk for taking and using.) The next day will be pouring with rain, the poll tax demands will have come shooting through the letter box (together with the electricity and gas bills), and everything will all at once seem nasty and gloomy.

These smokers have not managed to give up because they haven't understood what giving up involves. They haven't concentrated hard on any of the things which need to be considered and have not learnt how to become single-minded about the issue.

Time after time, people give up for a day or two and then revert to smoking because they haven't prepared themselves. Mark Twain himself said he had given up smoking thousands of times. Giving up instantly, without any thought or preparation, leads nowhere.

Although it is true that a few, almost super-human beings, have managed this way, it is also true that well over 95 per cent of those who try to give up instantly have not succeeded. Don't bother with this method. It's not worth the effort and upset.

Time to give up

Having read the previous chapters and done the exercises, it is time to give up. By now, you should be single-minded. That means that not only have you made up your mind to stop smoking but you are determined to do so and to succeed. You have thought long and hard, and all your thoughts should agree.

Now you have to decide *how* to give up. Some methods of giving up are set out below. It is for you to choose which method you think will suit you best. In order for you to make up your mind about which to choose, read through each method carefully and think hard about which you consider will be the easiest to manage. The methods are not easy, but then they are not impossible, either.

You might want to know which method is best to avoid withdrawal symptoms. Unfortunately, not enough is yet known about the addiction to, and withdrawal from, nicotine to say which is the best method from that point of view.

What does seem to be the case is that withdrawal appears not to be directly related to the number of cigarettes you have smoked a day. Thus, for example, someone who smokes sixty cigarettes a day (three packets) may be just as able to give up instantly as someone who smokes only ten a day.

Giving up cold turkey

Giving up cold turkey means quite simply that, after smoking your usual amount of cigarettes or cigars or pipe during the day, at some point in time, determined beforehand, you have a last smoke and then never smoke again. Surprising though it may seem, well over 80 per cent of all those who do give up, give up this way.

Apart from being recommended to those who smoke cigarettes, this method is the only one advocated for cigar and pipe smokers simply because cigar and pipe smokers smoke on far fewer occasions throughout the day than cigarette smokers, so the gradual reduction method is less appropriate – some cigar and pipe smokers only smoke two or three times a day.

ACTION

1   Well in advance, decide exactly what day and at what time you will have your last smoke. 'Well in advance' must mean some realistic date in the near future. It definitely does not mean 'tomorrow', because you won't have had time to work anything through. (Anyway, remember that tomorrow never comes.)

Equally, this does not imply some vague date in the unknown (and therefore un-thought about) future. It is no good saying 'I'll give up when I've got some time to really think about what I'm doing', or 'I can't think about anything constructive until I'm having my next holiday'. Make time, now, to think hard about when to give up smoking, even though you may not have a holiday for a year or so.

'Well in advance' does, however, mean sometime after the next two weeks but before a month is out. You will need at least two weeks to prepare yourself before giving up. This does not include the time you will have spent reading the introduction and first four chapters of this book and doing the exercises. It is essential that you and you alone choose the date and time to stop. Don't let anyone else do this for you or interfere in any way with your decision-maker. Remember, you are in charge.

2   For two weeks before you give up, in addition to the exercises outlined in chapters 1 to 4 which you will be doing every day, please do the following exercise twice a day. The first time should be as soon as you wake up in the morning, before you get out of bed, and the last time when you've got

into bed at night, just before you go to sleep.

(a) Lie in bed, flat on your back with your hands by your sides, and close your eyes.

(b) Say the following words out loud five times:
'I love my body and I love my mind. I am going to care for myself by giving up smoking. I shall give up smoking because I am determined. I will succeed because I have a single purpose in mind.'

(c) Now lie still for as long as it takes you to relax every part of your body. Try to relax your mind as well. Don't think about anything in particular.

The entire exercise should not take more than five minutes. Please don't treat it with scorn. Try to really mean what you say. At first it may be rather difficult to talk out loud – talking aloud and hearing oneself speak is part of the exercise – but persevere and this will become easier.

3 After two weeks you are now ready to give up. You know the day and the time when you are going to have your last smoke. Have it in peace, with no regrets and no fear for the future.

Once you have finished your last smoke you have given up smoking. It's no big deal. That's it. No fireworks, no crashing cymbals. Remember: no grief or feeling sorry for yourself. This is a time for gentle joy and relief. You've got there, and you've done it. It is the time for a change in your life, but nothing very dramatic.

Once you have given up you will probably experience withdrawal symptoms. For help with these and other difficulties associated with giving up smoking, please read chapters 6 to 10 of this book.

Giving up gradually

This is a somewhat different method. Only about 15 per cent of all those who give up, give up this way. Although at first sight it seems easier and not so drastic as giving up cold turkey, in fact it requires even more self-determination than giving up all at once. You have to have a will of iron.

The method also requires quite a lot more time and a very rigid adherence to schedules. Whatever you do, please do not skip any of the action points listed below.

Giving up gradually is not recommended for cigar and pipe smokers (see page 56). The actions listed below are for cigarette smokers only.

ACTION

1   Decide on the day you will start to give up. This should be sometime after the following two weeks but within one month.

2   Immediately after you have decided the date when you will start to give up, please begin to keep a diary of your smoking habits.

   The diary will be very important for you. It is going to help you decide what cigarettes to give up and when. Whatever you do, do not stop keeping this diary. You must write it up, every day, until you finally give up.

   List each one of the cigarettes you smoke, when it is smoked, and how important you rate it. By important, I mean whether or not the cigarette gave you some pleasure, or if it succeeded in acting as a prop, or whether it was effective as a barrier against other people, and so on. You might not have even been aware you were smoking, until you found yourself stubbing out the butt end in the ash-tray.

So that you don't forget, make a habit of jotting down the number of the cigarette, the time and its importance, immediately after you have stubbed it out.

Keep an exact record of the time. Have a five-star rating system. Thus:

*　　　　haven't really noticed smoking
**　　　 not at all important
***　　　moderately important
****　　quite important
*****　 important

If you can't rate the cigarette's importance, put one star. If you don't know how important it is to you, it can't be very crucial to your life.

An example of one day in a 'smoking diary' is set out below. Please note this is only an example and that your own pattern of smoking may be very different. You may smoke much more than this number or considerably less, and you may smoke at very different times.

Monday 5 April

Number	Time	Rating
1	7.00 a.m.	*****
2	7.36 a.m.	**
3	9.05 a.m.	***
4	9.50 a.m.	*
5	11.03 a.m.	****
6	12.06 p.m.	***
7	12.46 p.m.	*
8	2.39 p.m.	****

9	3.02 p.m.	**
10	4.36 p.m.	**
11	5.03 p.m.	*
12	7.11 p.m.	****
13	8.05 p.m.	*
14	9.36 p.m.	**
15	11.06 p.m.	***

3 On the fifteenth day after you started to keep a 'smoking diary', look carefully at what you have put down. You will almost certainly find that while your consumption of cigarettes may vary slightly each day, it won't in fact vary all that much. You will probably notice that there will be set times of the day when you light up, no matter what day of the week it is. In addition it is probable that the important cigarettes of the day will tend to be very much at the same time of the day each day, while the less important or unimportant cigarettes will be smoked at any time.

4 You are now going to work out the average number of cigarettes you have smoked in the last fortnight. Do this by adding up the total number smoked and then dividing that number by fourteen. (For the sake of simplicity, let us assume that you have smoked 210 cigarettes in fourteen days. Divide this by fourteen. The average number you have smoked is therefore fifteen.)

5 Having found out the average number of cigarettes you have smoked in the last fortnight, you will use this number as your starting point for gradually cutting down the number you smoke a day.

6 The time for starting to give up should be soon, now. Every day until you start to give up, think positively about doing this. Think how good it is going to be. Look forward to the day when you will start to give up with pleasure.

7   To help you think positively, do the exercise set out on p. 58 for those who are giving up cold turkey. Do this every day until you have smoked your last cigarette.

Continue each day with the 'smoking diary' but unless you feel like it there is no need to examine the diary in detail again until the day comes for you to start to give up.

8   On the day you have decided to start giving up, take the average number of cigarettes you have smoked per day over the fourteen-day period which you checked previously, and cut it by five. This is the number of cigarettes you will smoke per day for the next week.

For example, if the average number of cigarettes was fifteen, you are going to smoke only ten a day for the next week. If the average was twenty-five, you will smoke twenty, and so on. *From now on you must smoke an exact number of cigarettes a day, and this number must be the same number each day for the next seven days.* This is vitally important.

9   You must decide exactly how you are going to cut down, or, to put it a more positive way, how you are going to smoke not more than the given number of cigarettes. It is for you to choose which cigarettes you are going to cut out.

This is where your diary is going to help you. Look at it again very carefully. What cigarettes can you avoid smoking without any problems? Almost certainly, they will be the ones listed with only a one-star rating. Remember, you now have to plan your smoking day ahead of time. If you don't plan you are liable to end up having smoked your last cigarette by the early evening, and for late night smokers that just won't do at all.

Do remember to continue to note down all the cigarettes smoked, the time they were smoked and rate them on your five-point scale.

10 After seven days, cut out another five cigarettes each day, for a further seven days. If you were smoking ten per day, you will now be smoking five. Again, the ones you cut out are for you to choose. Use your 'smoking diary' to help you plan the day's smoking ahead of time.

Most people who smoke cigarettes do not smoke more than a packet a day, so by the time you have reached the end of the second week of gradually giving up, it is likely that most of the cigarettes you are now smoking you rate as quite important or important. Your 'smoking diary' will probably have changed quite radically.

This is not surprising. Very probably, you are now undergoing nicotine withdrawal symptoms, as well as a change in the habits you have formed over the period you have smoked. (Please see chapters 6 to 10, pp. 68–114, for help with withdrawal symptoms and other difficulties with giving up smoking.) It may appear that each cigarette seems like an oasis in a desert, a big thank God of relief. Please try very hard, however, to think in a different way to this. Try to think of all the good things that are happening to you. Your body is gradually being relieved of a terrible burden of poison and your mind is being freed from its enslavement to tobacco. *Think positively*.

11 At the beginning of the next seven-day period, cut out a further five cigarettes, and continue to cut out five a week, until you are down to five a day or less.

12 By the time you come to the last week, you will have five or

less cigarettes to smoke. Maybe you will be smoking only one cigarette a day. This will probably mean that your diary planning is now very important to you. Try not to make a big issue out of it. Endeavour to be as matter-of-fact as possible. With your last few cigarettes try very hard indeed to look forward to the time when you will no longer have to stand for the waste of time and sheer nuisance of planning your smoking day first thing in the morning, noting all the cigarettes smoked during the day, etc. etc. All the mess, the dirt, etc.

By this time you are almost certainly feeling – and almost undoubtedly are – much fitter. To help you relax and cope better with the withdrawal symptoms, do the following breathing exercise. Under no circumstances do this while you are smoking a cigarette.

(a) Lie down flat on your back on the floor.
(b) Breathe in deeply.
(c) Hold your breath and count to ten.
(d) Let your breath out slowly.
(e) Repeat this ten times.
(f) Lie quietly, breathing naturally, for one minute.

(**Warning:** Please do not do this exercise unless you are smoking less than ten cigarettes a day. If you do, it might be dangerous for you, putting unusual pressure on your heart and lungs and leading to a possible heart attack or angina. It is also not recommended for those who have given up cold turkey until they have stopped smoking for at least a month.)

The exercise should not take more than five minutes to do. It will help a great deal to make you relaxed.

13 Once you have reached the end of the week when you only have five or less cigarettes to smoke, you have finished. That's it. The sky won't fall in and it is not the end of the world. It is simply another day. Make sure it is a day of quiet joy and not one of mourning. There should be no fear of what the future will hold, only a determination that things will change for the better.

How to give up suddenly

You may have to give up smoking suddenly without any preparation. This could be for any one of a number of reasons. For example, you may be under doctor's orders to give up to prepare for an imminent operation, or you may be abruptly landed without any money. In any event, you will be in some degree of shock because of what has unexpectedly happened to you.

Perhaps you didn't have to give up but that, owing to particular circumstances, you've actually given up voluntarily. You may, for instance, have flu, and find that the taste of a cigarette has suddenly turned into something terrible. Or, that the combination of a bad cold and smoker's cough has meant that you are coughing so much and for such long periods at a time that you simply dare not have even just one, tiny puff. It could just be that pressure from other people, or pressure from the back of your mind which has been rumbling around for some time, makes you one day decide quite firmly and in a very matter-of-fact way to give up.

The thing to do is to capitalize on what you have done and to ensure that you do not return to smoking.

Whatever the reasons for giving up suddenly without any preparation, it is suggested you take the following action.

ACTION

1 Try to read the introduction and first four chapters of this book and do the exercises which are described.

Whatever you do, once you have stopped don't panic or say you can't manage without smoking. Instead, try to be as calm as possible under the circumstances, and be positive. Say to yourself that you have given up smoking – without any regrets or fuss.

2 From the time you give up and for the next three months, please do the following exercise twice a day. It is similar to the one for smokers giving up cold turkey.

The exercise should be performed for the first time as soon as you wake up in the morning, before you get out of bed, and the last time when you've got into bed at night, just before you go to sleep.

(a) Lie in bed, flat on your back, and close your eyes.

(b) Say the following words out loud five times:
'I love my body and I love my mind. I am caring for myself by having given up smoking. I have given up smoking because I am determined. I am succeeding because I have a single purpose in mind.'

At first you may think these words are meaningless. You probably haven't thought much about smoking, let alone about giving up. You haven't considered your body or your mind, while the need to care for yourself has possibly never even entered your head. As for your thoughts, they are probably all shrieking around in a jumbled mass. This is the time when these things have to be thought about, and fast. If you really concentrate on what you are saying, *and mean it*, your success in giving up will be assured.

    (c)   After you have finished saying the words, lie still for as long as it takes you to relax every part of your body. Try to relax your mind as well. Don't think about anything in particular.

A method of giving up which is not recommended

There is one method of giving up used by ex-smokers and written about elsewhere which I cannot recommend. This is aversion therapy, which is smoking to make yourself feel sick to try to alter the way you perceive smoking.

This method is dangerous. If you have a weak heart and pains in the chest (angina), these are very likely to get worse, and you might suffer a heart attack or even a stroke. If you find it difficult to breathe properly, by smoking a lot more the difficulties will get worse.

It has also proved to be not very successful. Using this method, the mind is supposed to equate smoking with feeling sick, but, as noted in earlier chapters, the mind plays very many tricks on smokers and the aversion may very soon be forgotten.

In addition to all this, aversion therapy, quite apart from being very unkind to your body and punishing your mind, runs contrary to the methods outlined in this book, which are all about reasoned persuasion and positive thinking.

SIX

Withdrawal Symptoms

When you stop smoking or cut down the amount you smoke each day, your mind and body have to adapt to the changes you are making.

Your body begins to manage better; it starts to deal more efficiently with the poisons you have been pumping into it. Your mind should be helping your body by being single-minded about the desire to stop smoking, by feeling relief at what you are doing and by looking forward to the future. It is essential that, while you are cutting down the amount you smoke each day or immediately after you have given up, you think positively. If you do this, *however* bad the withdrawal symptoms, *you will manage*. Think positive and be determined to succeed in what you set out to do.

What are withdrawal symptoms?

Withdrawal symptoms, sometimes called side effects, are sensations and feelings experienced when you give up smoking. Physical and psychological changes take place. Your body chemistry is adjusting to a drop in the bloodstream's nicotine level, while your mind is adjusting to being without dependence on the nicotine. Most, but not all, withdrawal symptoms are related to giving up dependence on the nicotine.

How bad is it going to be?

At the present time, not all that much is understood about withdrawal symptoms and why it is that while a few people suffer quite bad side effects, *up to one-third of all ex-smokers experience no ill effects at all*. You may very well be one of the lucky ones, in which case you can skip this chapter and chapter 7 and go straight on to chapter 8 (p. 86).

Most people who give up smoking experience some withdrawal symptoms, but very few have great difficulties. The first three days after you stop smoking are usually the most trying.

How badly you experience withdrawal symptoms does not seem to be related to how much you smoked a day. Someone who smoked three packets of cigarettes a day may have no symptoms, whereas someone who smoked only ten cigarettes a day may find life difficult for a short time. Smoking affects each of us in very different ways.

Those who quit smoking gradually may experience more side effects than those who quit cold turkey (see chapter 5, p. 54). Continued smoking may result in prolonged withdrawal symptoms, whereas stopping completely may result in a fairly rapid decrease of side effects.

A great deal depends on your attitude towards giving up. If you really want to do it and are determined, you will almost certainly have no trouble. But if you are looking backwards all the time, and regretting the necessary changes while feeling very sorry for yourself, you will find it very difficult to win through. *If you are committed to quitting you won't find difficulty in doing it.*

Things to remember

Before listing the withdrawal symptoms, there are a number of very important points to bear in mind. Please read these carefully and take note.

1 The withdrawal symptoms will not last for very long. Usually not more than three weeks at the most.

2 Never anticipate withdrawal symptoms. They may never happen.

3 Never have any reservations or lack of resolve about giving up.

4 Be positive. Never think that you hope you might be able to make it because you ought to. Always think that you want to stop smoking, you've done it, and that's that!

5 Do try to stay cheerful through all the changes and stress these changes may cause. Try if you possibly can to laugh at yourself. You will feel better if you do so. It is absolutely no good wallowing in self-pity and nostalgia. Why feel nostalgic about attempting to commit a long drawn-out suicide?

6 You have nothing to give up except poisoning yourself.

7 No one has ever died from giving up smoking.

The symptoms

The symptoms you might experience are listed below. Please bear in mind they are only what you might experience and that you certainly won't experience them all. You might not experience *any* of them.

Cravings For the most part these are linked to withdrawal from the nicotine. It is possible that nicotine affects the pleasure centre of the brain, so that cravings are partly mental as well as physical.

If cravings occur, they usually come in bouts and spasms which reach a climax. Each craving will last for no more than a few minutes, three at the most. It will then go away completely. Cravings occur mostly between twenty-four to forty-eight hours after stopping smoking and then decline in number and intensity.

After about three weeks, 99 per cent of the nicotine has left your body. If cravings persist after this time, they will be mental, not physical.

If you are giving up gradually and have reached the point where you are smoking ten or less cigarettes a day, you may experience some cravings which are not very intense. Do not, under any circumstances, smoke more cigarettes than your allotted number. If you feel you cannot manage, switch to the cold turkey method of giving up (see chapter 5, p. 56) and stop smoking completely. That way, though things may be worse for a few days, they will be easier sooner than if you continue to give up gradually.

ACTION

1   Don't sit with nothing to do.
2   Go for a walk.
3   Drink a glass of water. Take frequent small sips.
4   Do the following muscle relaxation exercise before meals or two hours after meals.

    (a)   Lie down on the floor on your back, with your legs straight down, heels on the floor and arms down the sides of your body.
    (b)   Close your eyes.
    (c)   Tense your jaw muscles rigid. Hold this position while you count to ten.
    (d)   Relax and breathe normally for fifteen seconds.
    (e)   Tense your neck muscles.

(f)   Relax and breathe normally for fifteen seconds.

(g)   Do the same with as many parts of the body as you can think of and which you have time for, or until you feel relaxed enough to cope with the cravings.

This deep muscle relaxation exercise has proved very helpful in coping with stress. If you do it at least twice a day, tensing and then relaxing many parts of the body, you will probably be able to sleep well at night.

Depression   You may feel extremely depressed after you give up and feel life is pointless. This may be experienced as a huge gap, a feeling of emptiness, or with being at a loss for something to do or say. Depression is linked to feelings of *anxiety*, when you feel that by quitting your whole world is caving in.

Most probably, if you experience these feelings, you have been using smoking as a prop, as something to help you cope with a none too friendly or easy world. As you know by now, smoking actually stops you coping.

ACTION

1   Do the deep muscle relaxation exercise set out above.

2   If this is no use, read the next chapter (chapter 7) which lists other things which might help, or phone either ASH or QUIT for further advice (see pp. 117–19).

3   Even though you may feel it is the end of the world, please hold on to the fact that you can give up.

Irritability and anger   When you give up smoking you are going through chemical and psychological changes. The balance of your physical and mental life has been disturbed. Smoking represses energy, which is now coming out as a negative force. Once you have given up for good, the irritability and anger should cease within one month.

ACTION

1   Try to use this energy as constructively as you can. Do things: take walks, write letters, learn another language.
2   Try not to upset other people. Right now, you can hardly help being a bit of a bull in a china shop, so do tell people who you have to be with that you are not your normal, sweet-natured agreeable self. If they themselves are reasonable people, they will understand. If not, try to avoid them.
3   A good way to vent your frustrations is to do the following exercise, which will also help you to deal with the cravings.

   (a)   Find a room by yourself where you can't be disturbed; you will probably have to do this at home in the evening.
   (b)   Get hold of a hard cushion.
   (c)   Pretend the cushion is someone you feel angry with.
   (d)   Sock the cushion. Go on. Get your anger out.
   (e)   Scream and yell and rage for as long as you like, and tell the cushion what a . . . he or she is. Continue until you are exhausted, or can't think of anything more to say.

Coughing   As soon as you give up completely, or have cut down a great deal, you may well find that your smoker's cough actually seems to get worse, rather than better. If you haven't had a cough, you may now start to get one.

The reason for this is that the cilia in the respiratory tract stop being paralysed and start to work again. They are now performing their natural function, which is to get you to cough up the mucus formed by the tar in the lungs.

ACTION

1 Don't take any medicines for this cough. It is good that it should happen. It means that everything is working well and is getting back to normal.
2 If, however, the cough continues after you have stopped smoking completely for more than two weeks, please see your doctor. In this case, it may be due to something other than the cilia working again.

Insomnia and sleep disturbances You may find it difficult to sleep for the first fortnight after giving up smoking. You may also have disturbing dreams. It is very common to dream of smoking; it is the mind's way of dealing with the changes that are taking place. When you wake up, have a good, long laugh. The smoke you had in your dream was the only safe one you ever had in your life.

ACTION

To help with insomnia:

1 Go to bed earlier, not later, than usual.
2 Drink a cup of hot milk just before going to bed.
3 If you wake up during the night, don't count sheep. Read a book instead.
4 If insomnia persists for more than two weeks after you have given up completely, phone ASH or QUIT for more advice (pp. 117–19).

Lack of energy and exhaustion You are withdrawing from nicotine, a stimulant which increases both the heart rate and blood pressure. As a smoker, you were constantly revving yourself up. Nicotine stimulates the central nervous system and adrenal glands. Both body and mind become adapted to the drug which you not only tolerated but needed to stabilize yourself with.

As you withdraw from the stimulant, your energy levels are depleted.

ACTION

1 Eat a balanced diet (p. 90) and take regular exercise.
2 Remember that you will soon have far more energy and be able to concentrate far better than you ever did while you were smoking.

Overeating. This is quite common when you stop smoking and the reasons are fairly simple. Your taste buds and sense of smell are getting much better and sharper and you feel hungry, perhaps for the first time for many years. The cravings for nicotine may also be very easily confused with pangs of hunger. The need to put something in the mouth to compensate for the lack of cigarette, cigar or pipe may be very strong.

Overeating may immediately make you feel bloated and rather sick, particularly if you are constipated (see below). It may, of course, rather quickly result in a weight gain which is probably not a good idea.

ACTION

1 Be very careful with what, and how much, you eat and drink.
2 If you feel the need for something in the mouth, chew gum.
3 See chapters 7 and 8 (pp. 78–94) for further suggestions about diet and what to put in the mouth.

Constipation Nicotine acts as a stimulant to the bowel. Without nicotine, the bowel may slow down its function.

ACTION
1 Don't panic. You won't burst. You will become regular within a week or so.
2 Eat plenty of fruit, vegetables and cereals.
3 Remember the good old prunes – once a day.

Slowing down of body metabolism   Nicotine induces the body's metabolism to speed up to an abnormal rate. When it slows down again, the body takes longer to digest foods. This may be another cause of overweight.

Inability to concentrate and restlessness   These are very common symptoms which fairly heavy smokers experience every day if they go without smoking for more than half an hour or so. They are the direct result of dependence on nicotine and will disappear within three weeks of giving up smoking completely. After this time, you will be able to concentrate more, not less, and will fidget less, not more.
ACTION
Try the deep muscle relaxation exercise given earlier (see p. 71).

Mouth sores and skin odours   These occur because the body is finding as many ways as possible of ridding itself of all the poisons, fast. After a fortnight these symptoms will disappear completely.
ACTION
1 With the money you have saved from not buying tobacco, buy yourself lots of foam bath treatments. Choose the ones with built-in moisturizer to keep your skin soft.
2 Soak yourself in a hot bath with these treatments at least once a day and twice a day at weekends.

Dizziness This may happen because you are now taking more oxygen into your lungs. It will not last for more than a few days at the most.

Itching This is a fairly rare withdrawal symptom which should cease after a week.
ACTION
1 Try not to wear scratchy clothes.
2 Cut your nails so that if you do scratch you won't hurt yourself.
3 Take your mind off your body by being active physically. Swimming is a very good idea.

There are some very rare withdrawal symptoms which are experienced by only a very few who have given up smoking. They are: *muscle cramps*, *fainting*, *nausea* and *vomiting*. If you experience any of these symptoms, please phone either ASH or QUIT (see pp. 117–19) or seek advice from your doctor.

Conclusion
Take care of yourself, take courage and be absolutely determined. That way you will win through and really change your life for the better. The time when you are gradually cutting down, or immediately after you have finished with smoking, may well be difficult to manage. Take heart: millions have managed and millions more will manage to stop smoking. You are not alone.

SEVEN

Helping You Along the Way

This chapter is about things which might help you on the way to giving up. First, though, a word of warning. Nothing listed below can stop you smoking; only you can do that. Remember that you cannot get anyone or anything to do the job for you; you cannot rely on anyone or anything other than yourself. It is up to you.

Smoking cannot be cured. It is not a disease. Rather, it is learned behaviour which has to be un-learned. Using any aid is a waste of time unless you are sure you want to give up. If you are really committed to quitting you will almost certainly not need any help, in which case you can skip this chapter and go on to the next.

It may be, however, that you find the withdrawal symptoms hard to manage, in which case an aid might be of some use in helping you to keep to your commitment. If this is the case, it will be worth your while to read on.

Medication
There are nicotine substitutes available on prescription. Your GP will be able to advise you of a suitable one.

Herbal medications Various herbal medications to help with giving up smoking are available from health shops. Their effectiveness has not been proven.

Talk to someone in your local health food shop about what is available. Before making a purchase, find out what the particular product consists of and what side effects, if any, it may cause.

Tablets, sprays, gargles and mouthwashes

Using any one of these means that if you start to smoke, the taste will be very unpleasant – even with the first draw. The active ingredient is usually silver nitrate or potassium permanganate. In combination with tobacco smoke, these chemicals generate a foul taste in the mouth which should stop you smoking at once. As long as you don't smoke, they taste rather minty.

The effects last from between two and four hours, and it is suggested that if you are using any one of these aids, you use it throughout the day and evening. How well any of them work has never been properly tested.

You can buy these at most chemists. It may be that one will come highly recommended by the chemist or shop assistant.

Dummy cigarettes

These are made out of cardboard or plastic and usually look and feel like real smokes. They contain menthol. They are available from some chemists and specialist shops.

Herbal cigarettes

These smell and taste horrible. I know; I used to smoke them. Herbal cigarettes have been around for a long time, but not surprisingly have never found a large market. Made out of, for example, dandelions, lettuces, mint or rosemary, they look just like tobacco-based cigarettes. Although they are not addictive, because they don't contain nicotine, they are still harmful because they do contain tar, and carbon monoxide is released when you smoke.

Only smoke these if the withdrawal symptoms seem to be driving you out of your mind. In your right mind you probably wouldn't dream of smoking them! They are available from some chemists and specialist shops.

Nicotine chewing gum

In 1980, a chewing gum called Nicorette was introduced into the UK. When chewed, it releases nicotine in tiny doses which is absorbed into the bloodstream through the mucus membrane (the lining) in the mouth. It is kept between cheek and gum to permit the slow release of nicotine.

There are special ways to chew this gum – slowly and intermittently – with instructions provided on the packet. If you chew it like ordinary chewing gum it can make you feel sick. It has an unpleasant taste, and may give rise to a sore throat and increased salivation, although if by chance you accidentally swallow the gum there is no need to worry as the nicotine embedded within it will be inactivated in the stomach.

If you decide to use Nicorette as an aid to giving up smoking, please remember you will still be dependent on nicotine. Experience with the gum so far suggests that only a small and specialized group of smokers are likely to benefit from it. The gum should only be used by those who are really genuinely keen to stop smoking.

It is available on prescription only, so you will have to see your GP. The National Health Service does not provide a prescription for the chewing gum, so you will have to bear the full cost which currently (1990) is around £10 per month.

Ordinary chewing gum

This is the only aid which can be recommended without reservations. Chew to your heart's content for as long as you like. Bear in mind the chewing gum will probably make you salivate and you may feel hungry sooner than you might want to.

There are many types of chewing gum available from most stores. A low sugar brand is particularly recommended.

Acupuncture

If you have acupuncture to help you to stop smoking, do heed the warning at the beginning of this chapter: *there is no cure because smoking is not a disease.* Many people have this treatment because they think an acupuncturist will stop them smoking. They are just wasting their time and money. Having said this, though, in some cases acupuncture has been found to produce a strong and immediate dislike for the taste or smell of tobacco.

To find an acupuncturist contact the British Acupuncture Association and Register who will provide you with a directory of all practitioners of acupuncture in the UK.

Hypnotherapy

Hypnosis is: 'the art by which a hypnotist induces a trance-like state of compliance and heightened suggestibility in another person.' Do remember that hypnosis cannot make you do anything if you don't want to do it, so you really have to want to be hypnotized before things can happen. Bear in mind that between 70 to 80 per cent of all subjects do not respond to hypnotherapy.

Ask yourself very firmly if hypnotherapy is what you want. Could it be that what you are really seeking is dependence on someone else? If you say to a hypnotherapist: 'I can't stop smoking; you do it for me', you will be asked to leave very quickly and, likely as not, charged a hefty fee without anything having happened.

The way people are induced to stop smoking by using the techniques of hypnosis vary from relaxed states to deep trance. There is almost no evidence available to show how effective this technique is.

If you are quite sure you want to try hypnotherapy, contact the National Council of Psychotherapists Hypnotherapy Register. Alternatively, some GPs offer hypnotherapy or are able to refer you to a registered hypnotist.

Moral support groups

Why don't you quit with other people? That way, it is a less lonely occupation. You can spend time together and counsel one another. You can also set up a telephone hot line and make an agreement that before you light up you will phone for support.

If you form a group, arrange to meet on a regular basis. Agree from the start never to smoke at these meetings. Before arranging a date when you will all quit together, you must all be quite sure that you really want to quit. Read about the dangers of smoking and the good things which will happen when you give up. Find out why each of you started to smoke and why you smoke now.

You will have to do a lot of talking through things to make sure you are all committed. If there is one member who is not really sure, he or she is likely to break up the group. Make a collective commitment to quit and agree on how you are going to quit, either cold turkey or gradually (see chapter 5, pp. 56–65). Then agree on a date when you will all quit, or start to quit, together.

Once you have all stopped smoking, *don't* stop seeing each other. Keep in close contact for at least six months afterwards and talk through the difficulties each of you has experienced. Probably you will find you have shared many of the problems.

You may well find that not only do you gain strength from the determination of others in the group, but that you yourself are helping others. Commitment is catching!

You may wish to start up a group with friends who also want to stop smoking. But if you don't know anyone else and wish to quit with a group, either phone your local health education unit (in your phone book under the name of the local health authority), or phone QUIT (see p. 119).

Anti-smoking clinics

Five-day smoking clinics   There are a number of anti-smoking clinics, originally devised and run by the Seventh-Day Adventist Church as a community service in the UK. The five evening meetings comprise a mixture of information about smoking and exhortation to stop, combined with advice on changes in diet, physical exercise and social activities over the initial period of abstinence. The members of these groups are divided into mutually supportive pairs, known as 'buddies'.

Long-term smoking clinics   Groups of ten to twenty people meet once a week under guidance. Each person has to describe his or her smoking history. All members have to agree on a set date to stop smoking. Such clinics provide psychotherapy, group support and information.

For information about anti-smoking clinics, either contact your local health education unit (in your phone book under the name of the local health authority) or phone QUIT which runs about 200 anti-smoking clinics throughout the UK.

Health farms

These are places which specialize in various forms of therapy, including methods to stop smoking. There might be intensive weekend sessions; more likely, a week-long course will be provided. Treatments run by health farms are very expensive but may suit you if you can afford them.

Addresses and telephone numbers of health farms may be found in health magazines. For further information, contact your local health food shop.

Action on Smoking and Health (ASH)

This organization was established in 1971 by the Royal College of Physicians. It co-ordinates voluntary action against smoking and provides the main bulwark of opposition against the tobacco lobby. ASH gives information and advice on how to give up smoking. Literature is also provided – apply in writing to the address listed on page 117.

National Society of Non-Smokers (QUIT)

Established as long ago as 1926, this organization helps people to stop smoking. It runs the National No Smoking Day. Information is provided over the telephone. QUIT co-ordinates the running of quit smoking groups which have been set up throughout the UK and provides counselling and help in the workplace as well as project ideas and information specifically designed for children.

The addresses and telephone numbers of all the organizations listed in this chapter are set out at the end of this book (see pp. 117–20).

EIGHT

Changing the Habits

Over the years, smokers form, and become attached to, very strong habits.

Those who don't smoke very much are usually quite fussy about just when they smoke (they wouldn't dream of smoking before breakfast) or where they smoke (they would be horrified with the idea of puffing away in the bath). They know exactly when and where to smoke. Light smokers also need to have nice things to use with smoking: a good-looking lighter, a rare pipe, an ash-tray given by a loved one. For them, the time has to be right, the place has to be right and things have to be right.

Heavy smokers, however, are not so fussy. They tend to grab at the first box of matches they find and light up at any time of day or night – even if this is in bed at four in the morning. However, they have still formed very strong habits attached to smoking: what they do when they smoke, and the way they move about with all the bits and pieces attached to smoking. Nevertheless, heavy smokers have certain set times during the day when bells go off in their heads to signify that it's time for a cigarette.

Getting rid of the trappings

The smoking gear must go. Not just the cigarettes, cigars and tobacco but all the bits and pieces that have to accompany the smoking: the pipes, the lighters, the matches, the filters, the ash-trays, the cigar-cutters, the pipe cleaners. They must not stay in their usual places, as the temptation to put them to use may be overwhelming. They should be out of sight and out of mind.

You must throw away the cigarettes and tobacco; if you can't throw or give away the lighters and ash-trays for sentimental reasons, bury them underneath some books or a mound of paper in a room you don't often use. Alternatively, put them in a box, inside some old boots or a jug which you don't like but which you can't throw away because your Aunt Esmarelda gave it to you for Christmas only five years ago. Make quite sure that all the paraphernalia related to smoking which you decide to keep is very difficult, if not impossible, to get at.

The smoking places

You also need to think about all the places you used to smoke in. Rearrange the furniture, so that the phone is in a different place, and when you sit down, sit in another chair so that you have a different view from the one that you have been used to. Make quite sure you also rearrange things as much as possible in your office – the pictures, your desk, where you sit – and get rid of all the ash-trays. Have it spring-cleaned and, if you can, repainted. These days, most bosses are very sympathetic to the needs of those giving up smoking, and you may get some unexpected, but very welcome, help from management.

When at home, spring-clean the entire house, especially the rooms where most of the smoking was carried out. There will be a dirty yellow-brown film, which not only looks, but smells, disgusting. Send all your clothes that you can't wash to the cleaners; have carpets and chair-covers cleaned; and re-paint the walls.

Changing daily routines

Change the time you do things. Get up later – you can afford to, now that you don't need that 7–10 minutes for the first smoke of the day. Have a bath in the evening rather than in the morning. Get out of the 'wrong' side of bed – never mind about superstitions. Eat a different breakfast: orange juice and cereal, for example, rather than coffee and toast. When you get to the bus, what ever you do, don't sit upstairs with the smokers.

Once at the office, arrange a different schedule to the one you normally have in the early morning. During the lunch break, eat slowly; there is no need to gobble the food down as if it were your last meal. Remember, there is no hurry. Think of all the time you are saving by not smoking! But, at the same time, make sure you always have plenty of work to do. Never have more time than you know what to do with or you'll be all the more likely to give in to the craving for nicotine.

Before you go home, plan carefully what you are going to do in the evening every day for the first three months after you have stopped smoking. Make quite sure this does not include very much sitting around watching television. There are plenty of other things to do which are much more enjoyable. What about going to see one of those many friends you haven't seen in a long time? How about going to the cinema or football match? (The pub is not such a good idea.)

There are also, of course, the rather less enjoyable tasks, like mowing the lawn, cleaning the car, tidying up the bathroom cupboard – all those things which don't have to be done today but which will have to be done sometime. Why don't you agree with yourself to do one of these jobs for, say, half an hour? Then stop at once. You'll feel so proud of what you have done that you'll want to continue the job the next evening.

Using the hands

If you are someone who liked to fondle cigars or cigarettes and miss this, fiddle with something else instead. Nobody is going to hold it against you or think you are something funny if you play with some worry beads. In fact, like as not you will be given some by sympathetic friends. Otherwise, why not try moulding bits of blue tack or plasticine, or scrunch up bits of paper into tight little balls? Have a large pad ready to draw lots of doodles with pen or pencil when the craving suddenly strikes.

Exercise

When you give up smoking, you have to learn to move differently, and the best way you can do this is by taking exercise.

Those who have smoked for many years are unlikely to be very energetic. Athletics and smoking do not go together, in spite of advertisements put out by tobacco companies suggesting that smoking is good for sport. If you've been a heavy smoker, the lungs are probably too clogged up to allow for very much movement at first. Now that you have stopped smoking it is important to start to get all parts of your body working again properly.

To begin with, don't do too much. For the first month walking a mile a day is quite sufficient. Gradually increase the amount if you can, and walk faster until your are doing a brisk three miles a day. Walk to the paper shop in the early morning to collect your newspaper, instead of having it delivered. If you have time, take a walk round the block during your lunch break. Take a walk in the evening after work; your dog will love you that much more.

How about starting to play tennis, or kicking a football

around in the park with the children? Less energetic sports include table tennis or badminton. Unless you have a heart condition, which means you have to take things carefully, almost any sport will do you good. To begin with, do take things easy. Remember, you are out of condition and all those muscles you have not used in years are going to protest about being suddenly called into action. Swimming is another very good idea, if you don't mind water! As well as giving you exercise it also helps you to relax, and will ease the tension caused by the withdrawal symptoms and changes in life style.

Eating and drinking

It is very important to keep a very careful eye on what you eat and drink and to make quite big changes in this part of your life.
Food   Do have three meals a day; cutting out a meal will not keep you slim. Don't have second helpings. Eat a balanced diet. Before you stop smoking, make sure you stock up with foods which are low in calories but high in fibre and nutrition. For instance, whole-grain breads, cereals and brown rice. You will also need to eat high protein foods such as fish, chicken, eggs and nuts. If you can bear to, eat lots of vegetables. (The best way to cook them is to steam them to preserve the goodness.) Eat all sorts of fruit and as much as you want. Try some of the many new varieties now available in large supermarkets.

Have the bare minimum of salt on your food, because you do not want to retain water.

Avoid the following: *red meat*, because it is suggested this helps you retain nicotine; *snacks*, because you want to stay slim. In this country avoiding snacks is very difficult, because we have all become used to buying a packet of crisps here and a chocolate bar there – to 'fill the gap'. This is partly because we are accustomed to eating a lot of meals with only short intervals in between. We start off with breakfast, then elevenses, then dinner, then tea, then supper – eating never seems to stop. Have substantial meals with nothing in between – and this means no snacks.

If you are absolutely desperate to pop something in your mouth, make sure whatever it is low in calories. How about a carrot which you can slowly munch, or a stick of celery?

Sugar should be avoided if at all possible because it is very fattening. If you can't give it up altogether, try very hard to cut down. For example, take only half a desertspoonful in a bowlful of cereal.

Sweets and chocolates should not be eaten because they are fattening and bad for the teeth. Be very careful, because they may become very tempting as substitutes for a smoke.

Drinks Drink plenty of non-alcoholic liquids. The more you drink, the quicker you can flush out all the poisonous substances retained from smoking. Why not try fresh apple, grapefruit or orange juices for a change? A nice warm mug of milk in the evening helps soothe the nerves – but don't drink this if you are prone to the snuffles or have sinus trouble. Herb teas may also help to calm you down.

Drink as little alcohol as possible. The more booze you consume, the more you begin to relax and the more likely it is that the defences you are beginning to build up against smoking will come tumbling down. After a few drinks, it becomes only too easy to accept a cigarette or cigar from a friend who offers you one with the words 'Go on! It won't hurt you, just one, this once!' It will hurt you, and you'll have to start to stop smoking all over again.

Quite apart from the temptation, remember, too, that you

are not your normal self. Alcohol will enhance your mood, which is very likely to be aggressive. Even when stone cold sober you will probably be somewhat moody, fraught and petulant, to put it mildly. With just a bit of beer, wine or spirits inside you, your friends most certainly will not want to know the raging Rottweiller showing its fangs, and liable to pounce without warning, that you've become. Be as sweet natured as you possibly can be under the circumstances and stick to the odd half pint or so. Make sure you keep the fridge stocked with fruit juices or mineral waters for you to drink as an alternative.

Avoid *Indian or China tea and coffee*, because you very probably strongly associate these two beverages with smoking. Studies have indicated that there might be a link between drinking large numbers of cups of coffee and excessive smoking. Also the tannin in tea and caffeine in coffee are not much good for you. You have to take great care of your body while you are going through all these enormous changes in your life.

Vitamins

For the first month after you stop smoking, you should treat yourself to lots of vitamins. You are not being a wimp or genteel in doing this. You need them to help you to cope with all the stress the major changes in your life have caused. The following vitamins are especially helpful: vitamin A, vitamin B_1 (thiamine), vitamin B_5 (pantothenicacid), vitamin B_6 (pyridoxine), vitamin C, and vitamin E. The B vitamins will help to calm you down and stop you getting too depressed, while vitamin C will give you lots of energy. Vitamin E can help render pollutants in your body harmless. Calcium tablets are also recommended to ease excessive stress.

Tips

1 **Get rid of the smoking gear**
2 **Attend to the smoking places**
    rearrange the furniture
    spring-clean and repaint rooms
    clean coverings and clothes
3 **Change daily routines**
    do things at different times
    eat different things
    always have something to do
    plan life out of office hours
4 **Use the hands**
    play with worry beads
    use other materials to keep the hands occupied
    draw doodles
5 **Take exercise**
6 **Change eating and drinking habits**
    eat three meals a day
    eat a balanced diet
    take little salt
    avoid red meat, snacks, sugar, sweets and chocolates
    drink lots of non-alcoholic drinks
    drink little alcohol
    avoid Indian or China tea and coffee
7 **Take vitamins**

ACTION
1 **First thing on the day after you have stopped smoking, do the following:**
    ● Throw away the smoking gear. Bury anything you can't throw away.

- Make a list of all the things you did while you smoked and the places you used to smoke in.
- Think of the times in the day which are going to be troublespots – when you will really want to smoke.
- Think of how you can change your routine to avoid these.
- Plan to do different things to what you usually do outside office hours.
- Plan changes in your diet (see p. 90).

2 **Later in the day:**
- Wash clothes or send them to the cleaners.
- Clean the furnishings.
- Rearrange the furniture.
- Buy vitamins (see p. 92).

3 **For the next three months:**
- Each day, carefully plan what you are going to do. Do not leave any time unaccounted for.
- When you have time, paint the rooms you smoked in.
- Each day, take some exercise. Take it gently at first, and each day do a little more.
- Change your diet and drinking habits (see p. 90).
- Take vitamins (see p. 92).

4 **For ever:**
- Always eat and drink in moderation and attend to your diet.
- Always take some exercise every day.

NINE

Associations and Temptations

After you stop smoking, for the first two or three months or so, there will probably be times of the day when you will want to smoke very badly indeed. This won't only be because of the withdrawal symptoms from the lack of nicotine, though for the first three weeks these play a very large part in the problem. The reasons for suddenly wanting a smoke have almost as much to do with the habits formed over long periods of time and the associations with smoking. This chapter is particularly related to the associations with smoking, and the temptations which follow.

Fortunately, the times when you most want to smoke are often predictable. Once you have been two days without smoking, you will know pretty well at what times of the day you want to light up and what you associate with this. For instance, smoking may be particularly associated with drinking, especially coffee, tea and alcoholic beverages (see chapter 8 and below).

Think hard about the times when you know you had a smoke. For instance, there is the first cigarette of the day which, if you are a heavy smoker, is usually shortly after waking up, before getting out of bed. Then there might be the cigarette after breakfast with a second cup of tea or coffee. There is almost certainly one with the mid-morning coffee break, and the one after the midday meal. Then the tea break, with a cigarette, and the early evening one with a drink. At night there is the after supper smoke and the last cigarette of the day. That is only eight. While not all cigarettes are a question of habit and association, a great many are.

The average number of cigarettes now smoked a day is around sixteen, but there are some smokers who smoke far less and only at set times. For example, those who smoke only in the morning – or only in the evening. Those who stick rigidly to five a day in the mistaken belief that this will save them from ill-health. There are also those who crazily suggest, when offered a packet: 'No thank you, I only smoke on special occasions'!

Cigars and pipes are usually smoked at very set times, too. Because there is more involved with lighting cigars and pipes, the smoker has to be in a relaxed and comfortable atmosphere, where he or she is not going to be bullied about the terrible smell and smoke created.

ACTION

In the evening of the second day after you have given up smoking, please do the following.

1 Make a list of everything which you particularly associate with smoking.
2 See if there is any way in which you can change your routine. Are there, for example, associations you could avoid so that the temptations to smoke are lessened? (Could you stop drinking coffee, tea and alcohol for a while?)
3 Think hard about these associations and how, if you cannot avoid these, you are going to deal with them. For example, if you cannot do without tea, coffee or alcohol, before you

drink, say to yourself the following 'I am not smoking any more, and it's wonderful!' Be positive and take charge. That way, you will win through, easily.

Some of the most common associations and temptations are listed in this chapter, but you are bound to have other bad times of your own. Take heart; you are not alone. All over the country, there are hundreds of people going through very much the same as you are at the present time.

The telephone

A major bugbear is the 'phone. If you don't have one in the home, the chances are you will be using one at the office.

As an instrument the 'phone causes stress. When it rings, you don't know who is on the other end of the line. While it might be a colleague telling you there is no photo-copying paper left, it equally might well be your mother saying she has fallen down stairs and has broken her leg. More likely, it could be an upset client demanding to know exactly why his order for goods has not yet been delivered as promised. When you make the call, while it might be just to order some sandwiches from the shop for lunch, it might also be to tell your partner that you can't make it home in time for the cinema because you have to work late.

Previously, when you heard the bell or wanted to use the 'phone yourself, it probably triggered something in your mind to the effect that it was time to light up to help with the stress. The nicotine would help you to concentrate and the withdrawal symptoms would cease. You had come to associate the 'phone with smoking. The 'phone equalled smoking. It was as simple as that.

Now it is no longer simple. You have to stop all those old associations with the 'phone.

ACTION

1 Whenever you use the 'phone have a glass of water with you. While using it, take small, fairly rapid, sips.

2 Before you pick up the 'phone, say to yourself: 'I have finished with smoking, and this is wonderful. I am in control.' *Really mean* this, with all your thoughts. Think positively.

3 Once connected, listen to the person at the other end of the line. Try not to think about smoking at all. Concentrate on what is being said as well as you can.

4 If it is a nasty 'phone call, brace yourself. You are in control and you don't need a prop. Listen carefully to what is being said and always reply politely. Don't let the person at the other end get you down. Never let yourself become a victim by shouting, or making excuses, or moaning.

5 The person at the other end just might be one of your jocular smoking friends, ringing up to find out how you are coping without smoking. Slowly and calmly, say that you are doing fine – and try to change the subject. Don't, whatever you do, say 'Oh, it's murder; life isn't worth living'! This is exactly what your smoking friend will want to hear. You will then somehow be pressurized to have just one to help you to calm down. Don't give in to this emotional blackmail. By being negative and feeling sorry for yourself you will have become the victim and the one who is being led. Most important of all, don't let yourself be bullied like this.

Smokers in the office

You may be the first non-smoker in an office. Suddenly you appear to be in the minority and an outcast. Rather than thinking like this, why not see yourself as being the leader? You have set the path which others will follow.

ACTION

1 If you are working in an office with other smokers, ask to change rooms. Tell your boss that you have given up smoking and do not want to be a passive smoker. These days, non-smokers are being listened to with a great deal more sympathy than they were ten years ago. Your boss will probably readily agree to your request.

2 If your boss doesn't agree, and you can't get anyone higher up the ladder to agree, you will have to be very firm with your smoking colleagues. Ask them to smoke when you are not around.

3 Talk gently but firmly with your colleagues. Never shout or scream or bang the table. Try to keep calm at all times. If they go on at you, answer back politely. Reason with them. You have reason on your side. Remember, it is your colleagues, not you, who are really suffering.

4 Make a point of opening the window to let in some fresh air.

Smokers at home

People smoking at home is a difficult problem to deal with. The smokers will feel irrationally betrayed by you joining the non-smoking camp. They may well try hard to re-convert you to smoking. Don't let them! Be firm. If the members of your family know you mean business, they will listen to what you have to say and treat both it and you with respect. It's amazing how people close to you (and not so close, for that matter) know instantly if you say something and really mean it. Nine times out of ten they will back off and let you have your way about what you want to do.

Don't lecture or hector smokers. They will almost certainly eventually follow your example, if you are quite sure you mean to continue not smoking. Smokers, deep down, know they are doing themselves, and others, harm by smoking, and they also know they are being weak-willed.

ACTION

1   Insist that all the smoking gear be put away once it has been used by the smokers, out of sight and out of mind. This is a reasonable request, not an erosion of others' rights.
2   Insist on as many rooms as possible being smoke-free.
3   Open windows to keep the house full of fresh air.
4   Buy lots of air-fresheners.
5   Ask that no one smokes in your presence. This, again, is a reasonable request.

Social smokers

As a smoker, very possibly you met up socially with other smokers. Smokers tend to huddle together against the rest of the world these days. This might be in a pub, wine bar or restaurant, where you are trapped by the smoke and can do nothing to stop it. The people you are with are your friends, whom you may have known for some time. You don't want to leave them, you cannot ask them to stop, but how can you get through the evening?

Having given up, you have changed. The rest of the group, who most definitely do not want change, will want you back in the smoking fold as soon as possible. They will try very hard to persuade you with such comments as 'Go on! Just one won't hurt!' or 'Come on, have one! You make us feel like lepers!', or: 'Stop being such a prig!' With this sort of pressure being applied, what do you do?

ACTION

1   If you possibly can, avoid seeing your friends for three weeks after you have given up smoking. By the time you do see them the withdrawal symptoms should have finished, so that it will be easier to manage being with them in conditions which you cannot control. You will also have more control over what you are doing and probably be more determined than ever not to go back.

2   Quietly but firmly refuse the offer of cigarettes or cigars.

3   Ask your friends to stop pestering you. You have made your decision and you are sticking by it.

4   If you are drinking, be very careful not to have very much alcohol. Preferably, don't drink any at all. Instead, have a glass of water or orange juice. Alcohol very quickly stops you thinking properly. After a few drinks, you are away, and things don't seem to matter any more. One puff from someone else's cigarette can't do any harm . . . then you're back again to where you started.

Temptations in the evenings

A time of day when the need to smoke may be pressing heavily is in the evening, when you've eaten, you're tired, you're just beginning to relax from a stressful day and you've put your feet up in front of the television. Then the withdrawal symptoms begin to nag – because you've nothing to take your mind off them. You become scratchy and restless. It is not only the withdrawal symptoms; it is also the habits and associations formed. Television equals smoking.

ACTION

1   Get up from your chair and do something else: go out of the house; write a letter; read a book; 'phone a friend. Best of

all, 'phone up someone who is giving up at the same time as you and talk out the need to smoke.

2 All the time, say to yourself and to others that you can manage. Be positive.

3 If you *have* to watch the television programme, try to concentrate on it as much as you can.

4 Have a glass of water near by and take frequent sips.

5 Every half hour, while you are watching television (match it up with the advertisements) do the following. Breathe in deeply. Hold it. Count to ten. Breath out, slowly. Do this ten times. This really does help you to relax and gets the lungs working again, properly. (**Warning:** this exercise is not recommended for those who have given up cold turkey until they have stopped smoking for at least a month. See chapter 5 p. 64.)

Give yourself a treat

After one week of not smoking, you will have been through many temptations. It will have been hard work to have stuck to your decision. So be nice to yourself and do or buy something special. You can afford to. You are going to save a lot of money (see chapter 2, p. 25).

So how about a Sunday trip to the seaside with the family? Or that sauna you always thought you might try out but never got round to? Why not go out to the shops and buy yourself some new clothes? If you like gardening why don't you pop off to a nursery and hunt around for your favourite flowers?

Giving up smoking means a whole new life and a different way of looking at things. You have to learn to be nice to yourself; you haven't been while you've been smoking. If you treat yourself well, you will feel good and so will others.

ACTION
1 Spend money on yourself. You deserve it!
2 Take a friend to see a film!
3 Buy some flowers for your bedroom.
4 Invite some friends round for a special dinner.
5 Take a long, relaxing bath.
6 Have breakfast in bed.
7 Plan an exotic summer holiday.

TEN

Smoking Affects Others

This chapter is about the dangers smoking causes to everyone – to those who don't smoke as well as to those who do. It is also about ways and means to encourage people not to smoke.

It is assumed that you have read the preceding chapters of this book and have become, or are about to become, an ex-smoker. Even if this is not the case, it is very much hoped that you now agree that smoking is not only anti-social but also harmful, and that every effort should be made to encourage smokers to stop.

Until about twenty years ago smoking was so pervasive, with many more adult smokers than non-smokers, that smokers assumed an implicit right to smoke. From around 1970, however, the number of smokers declined quite dramatically to the present figure of around 14 million (1990). This may sound like an enormous number of people, but not if you consider there are 11 million ex-smokers and around 30 million people who have never smoked.

Recently there have been many squeals from smokers who feel threatened and outraged because people who don't smoke, now in the majority, are demanding more bans on smoking and more smoke-free zones. Some smokers say they have a moral right to enjoy a habit they regard as pleasurable, that in a democratic country they have an inalienable right to smoke.

In February 1990, smoking became illegal on almost all domestic flights in the USA, and a very disgruntled and rather desparate traveller complained that 'somehow a bunch of sanctimonious wackos have managed to legalize torture'. Why sanctimonious, and who exactly is being tortured? There are many non-smokers who have no choice but to endure the unpleasant fumes of tobacco. It is not simply a question of 'one man's meat is another man's poison'. Smoking is a poison for everyone.

Long ago, King James I recognized this when he said of smoking that it was: 'Lothesome to the eye, hateful to the nose, harmful to the braine, dangerous to the lungs, and in the black stinking fume thereof nearest resembling the horrible Stigian smoke of the pit that is bottomlesse.'

Passive smoking

Passive smoking, sometimes referred to as 'involuntary' or 'second-hand' smoking, is breathing in other people's smoke. When a cigarette is smoked, the atmosphere becomes contaminated by two types of smoke: 'main stream' and 'side stream' smoke.

Main stream smoke is inhaled by the smoker and then exhaled into the air. Side stream smoke, which is not inhaled, is emitted from the burning cone of the cigarette between puffs. Most cigar and pipe smokers do not inhale, which means the main stream smoke is likely to be exhaled into the atmosphere with little modification.

Nearly 85 per cent of smoke in a room is side stream, and this is smoke which contains many toxic gases such as carbon monoxide and ammonia. There is no safe level of exposure, and the World Health Organization has made it quite clear that passive smokers should be protected against smoking, which it says is a noxious form of environmental pollution.

The effects of passive smoking

A non-smoker in a room full of smoke may inhale as much smoke in one hour as an average cigarette smoker inhales from one cigarette, and there is a very real possibility of some damage to health. The main risks are outlined below.

Smoke in the eyes Nicotine is an irritant to the eyes. (If a room is warm and dry, a humidifier often relieves the irritation.) Smoke also often affects vision.

Smoke up the nose Although the nose filters out up to 90 per cent of soluble gasses, including those in smoke from tobacco, some people suffer a dry nose, or the opposite, a nasal discharge. Others endure itchy noses, which they frequently rub. There is also, of course, the unpleasant smell, both of tobacco smoke and the breath of a smoker, which come together when the butt end is twisted out in an ash-tray.

Allergies to smoke A few people are geniuinely allergic to tobacco smoke, and will at once begin sneezing and coughing. They might get a headache and start itching. Such reactions, sometimes perceived as over-dramatic and hysterical by a few intolerant smokers, are in fact completely outside the control of the sufferer. In such circumstances, smoking should be stopped at once. There is also the danger that those who suffer from asthma might have an attack, particularly if they are trapped in a small, enclosed space (for example, a small office or car) with a chain-smoker.

Lung cancer There is a 35 per cent increase in the risk of lung cancer in non-smokers living with smokers. To date, passive smoking may have accounted for hundreds of deaths from lung cancer in the UK, though as yet there has been no in-depth study to verify this.

Heart disease For those who already have heart disease, a smoke-filled room may precipitate attacks of anginal pain.

Passive smokers at risk

There are those who are particularly vulnerable to the dangers of smoking. They have no say in what sort of environment they would prefer, the use and abuse of which is dictated by smokers.

Old people Old people are likely to be very vulnerable to the atmosphere. If it is contaminated, they will be affected. There are many well over the age of retirement who live in homes other than their own and cannot escape from their smoking companions – more to the point, they cannot avoid their smoke.

The foetus Pregnant women who smoke ten or more cigarettes after the fourth month of pregnancy tend to give birth to children who show poor progress at school up to the age of sixteen.

It is thought that nicotine may have an effect on the growing tissues of the foetus. In any event, babies weighing less than $5\frac{1}{2}$ lb (2.6 kg) at birth are nearly twice as common among mothers who smoke than among those who don't smoke.

Premature births are almost double the rate in women who smoke than in women who do not smoke. There is also a 30 per cent more likely occurrence of still birth or death in the first week of life in babies of mothers who smoke regularly after the fourth month of pregnancy.

A change in the foetal heart rate may occur with the mother smoking.

Children Mothers who breast feed and smoke pass on nicotine in their milk to their infants. Infants of parents who smoke develop poor lung function. They are more susceptible to chest infections, coughs, bronchitis and pneumonia. Respiratory illnesses are significantly more common in the first year of life, and there is also an increased incidence of middle-ear infection.

Children whose parents smoke are receiving the equivalent of eighty cigarettes a year *minimum*. They run a higher risk of cancer when they become adults than do children whose parents do not smoke.

Ways to discourage smoking

Though smokers are now in the minority, they are still polluting the atmosphere breathed in by everyone. It is the rights of passive smokers and not those of smokers which are being eroded.

Especially important is the effect of smoking on children. At the present time, more children, particularly more girls, are smoking than they were ten years ago. A few facts and figures will show the extent of the problem.

In 1984 children aged eleven to sixteen spent £90 million on smoking. Thirty-three per cent of regular smokers start before the age of nine. Currently (February 1990) at the age of fifteen, 18 per cent of boys and 27 per cent of girls are classified as smokers. About one in five children smoke and nearly one in ten are regular smokers, smoking an average of about fifty cigarettes a week. Studies show that more than 75 per cent of all current smokers start before their twenty-first birthday. Conversely, anyone who has reached the age of twenty and hasn't smoked is unlikely to begin.

About 80 per cent of children who smoke regularly continue to do so when they grow up. The earlier in life a person starts to smoke regularly, the greater the risk of early death. The last report on smoking by the Royal College of Physicians, published in 1983, said: 'if an advertising ban affected only the uptake of smoking by children, the ultimate benefit to mankind would be enormous, and the importance of introducing legislation to enact such a ban cannot be over-emphasized.'

It is therefore very important to find ways to encourage children not to smoke. Some suggestions are outlined below.

In the home   The main influence on children is people in the home. Very often it is parents who, themselves smokers, mistakenly think it is somehow 'right' and 'democratic' to allow their children to smoke. There have been many instances of parents openly encouraging their children to smoke by offering them cigarettes, even at the ages of nine or ten. In one survey, one-quarter of all ten to twelve-year olds interviewed said they were given their first cigarette by their parents.

Underlying this is probably the feeling the parents have of wanting their children to be doing what they do. If everyone is smoking there is less likelihood of feeling guilty or worrying about getting ill or in thinking what harm is being done to others not in on the act.

You may now, or might soon, be an ex-smoker. In any event, if you've read this book and are a parent, you will know that encouraging children to smoke may be, literally, fatal for them. Please don't do this. Instead, talk about the issue and tell your children that you have given, or are about to give, up. Tell them you now think differently to the way you used to. They will respect you for this.

Most parents who smoke, however, do encourage their

children not to smoke and sometimes punish their offspring quite severely if they catch them at it. Children are extremely logical creatures and are always quick to notice unfair behaviour. Why, they reason, are we told not to do something our parents do? Why should it be bad for us but nice and good for them? They may rapidly come to the conclusion that the ban on smoking for them is ridiculous, and just what the wrinklies would do, anyway.

Here, the parents are in a bind. They know, rightly, that smoking is bad for the health, and want to protect their children. Yet they continue to do themselves harm.

But if you as a parent have now changed, or are about to change to being an ex-smoker, your arguments will now hold far more weight. Your children will respect you for your actions and will listen to, and accept, your judgements.

There are some parents who believe that talking about smoking draws attention to the issue, and that this encourages their children to start. Alternatively, that if the parents themselves smoke, telling their children not to smoke sets a contrary example. In such households, smoking is a banned topic of conversation, and the subject becomes taboo, like sex. This can be curiously exciting. Not to say anything about smoking is almost as bad as condoning the practice.

Having read this book, you now know that it is really important to make sure the subject is discussed and argued about at length. The more information available to children, the less likely they will be to start to smoke.

Parents who don't smoke and who talk to their children about smoking, clearly outlining the dangers, are likely to have children who not only don't smoke but become quite militant against smoking.

At school   A school with an active no-smoking policy – that is, one which provides lectures, discussion groups and leaflets about the issue, and with teachers who don't smoke – is far more likely to have young adults leaving the school who don't smoke than a school with no such policy.

If your child attends a school which does not seem to be bothered about the smoking issue, write to the head teacher and ask for something to be done. Alternatively, write to the newly formed Parents Against Tobacco or ASH to ask for advice.

Selling tobacco products to children   If children are under the age of sixteen and are buying tobacco products (usually cigarettes), they are obtaining them illegally. Retailers often turn a blind eye to the law. For the owner of a corner shop, the sale of tobacco products is usually a lucrative part of their business which, in these days of super- and hypermarkets can be an increasingly risky venture.

Many retailers claim they don't know about the law, but it is really very simple. No child under the age of sixteen should be sold any tobacco product. The law should be more strictly enforced. Every effort should be made to encourage children not to smoke. If they continue with the practice, smoking will never be eradicated.

In general, retailers should set a better example and abide by the law. If a child comes into a shop asking for a packet of cigarettes yet seems to be much younger than the age of sixteen, the retailer should refuse a sale.

If you are a parent who still smokes, please don't ask your child to go up the road for a packet of cigarettes. Apart from being an unreasonable thing to ask of anyone, this is very likely to encourage him or her to smoke in the near future.

Information about smoking

At present, the information received by the general public from various sources about smoking is somewhat confused and contradictory. For instance, while the government has decreed a total ban on advertising cigarettes on television, advertisements for cigars and pipe tobacco are still allowed. Tobacco companies can advertise freely in most newspapers, journals and magazines, and on advertisement hoardings.

While smokers may know that smoking is not good for the health, with every packet of cigarettes and cigars containing a suitable warning, they may be reassured by, for instance, cosy advertisements, certain of which suggest that cigars are all about peace and comfort. Or by the fact that tobacco companies sponsor sporting activities and cultural functions, which erroneously suggest that smoking is somehow linked with healthy and respectable activities.

Promotion through advertising and sponsorship reinforces a favourable climate of opinion towards tobacco products and tends to make the efforts of health educators useless.

At present, £3 million of government money is spent each year in trying to encourage people to stop smoking. This may seem like a huge sum of money, but it is nothing in comparison to what tobacco companies spend, which is well over £100 million each year advertising their products in the UK alone.

Government policy is contradictory, mainly as a result of a lack of co-ordination within the various government departments. The government could, however, be very effective in helping to encourage people to stop smoking by banning all advertising of tobacco products and by increasing the amount of money provided for information about the real effects of smoking.

The amount of time, energy, talent and money previously spent by tobacco companies on persuading people to smoke could benefit smokers and ex-smokers by provision of research into cures for diseases caused by consumption of tobacco.

The tax on tobacco

A packet of cigarettes or cigars now (1990), costs less in real terms than it did in the mid-1950s. The annual revenue from the sale of tobacco is a very lucrative source of income, even though tobacco now accounts for only 4 per cent of total government revenue, rather than 16 per cent as in 1948. It is currently at a level of about £5,000 million. This is probably why the government appears to be cautious about taxing smoking out of existence.

The present tax on tobacco, which is the main factor affecting the price of a packet, is not nearly enough to discourage smokers to stop smoking. Don't you think it should be increased?

Things are getting better

It is not only non-smokers but also the majority of smokers who agree that the number and size of no-smoking areas should be increased.

In this country there are already non-smoking compartments in trains, buses and aeroplanes. British Rail have recently (1990) announced they are considering a total ban on smoking. Almost all theatres and some cinemas and restaurants have a no-smoking policy.

Recently, there has been a significant shift towards a ban on smoking in offices. To save on energy, buildings built within the last twenty years have been made air-tight. Unfortunately, the lack of air exchange causes an accumulation of cigarette smoke. Managements have calculated the cost in terms of days off taken by all personnel as a result of ill-health, and it adds up to too much. It is estimated that 50 million working days a year are lost through illness caused by smoking.

Some organizations ban smoking completely; there are more which have set aside smoking rooms. Those who want to smoke have to clock off work, make a trek to the smoking room, have a smoke, and then go back to work. The inconvenience is deliberate, and very recent studies have suggested that such a policy is resulting in smokers cutting down quite considerably.

With more smoke-free areas, both the number of times and occasions where people are able to smoke are reduced. For example, those who used to smoke travelling to and from work on the London Underground can now no longer do so. Smoking is now banned, which means smokers now have two enforced breaks from smoking which did not happen when smoking was allowed on the tube. This does not mean they will make up for their lack of smoking by smoking more later. What it does mean, however, is that, with less smoking, smokers are relatively more healthy and passive smokers are relatively less affected – and overall there is less pollution of the atmosphere.

With more smoke-free areas there is an increasing awareness on the part of smokers that their smoking affects others and is antisocial. With increased awareness, the pressure for more smoke-free areas will grow.

Conclusion

When you read this, you will probably have read the rest of the book. It is also very much hoped you will have given up smoking.

The Royal College of Physicians says that the longer you can manage to go without smoking, the easier it becomes. Not only that, but the risks of ill-health become ever more similar to those of people who have never smoked.

After the first few weeks, when the withdrawal symptoms (if any) have finished, and you are breaking the habits and associations with smoking, please continue to be on guard against complacency and over-confidence. There are many who, once they have stopped smoking for about a month, think: 'Well, that's that; I've done it; now I can turn to other things.'

However, it really isn't quite so simple. *Always* watch out for people offering you a cigarette. Often, without thinking, you may suddenly find yourself in a tobacconist's shop, about to buy a packet – even though you are no longer physically dependent on the nicotine. As you well know by now, the mind can play strange tricks.

All of us ex-smokers have to remember, and most especially when we are sorely tempted to join in with our smoking friends' occupation, that we are only one smoke away from once more being a smoker. We are, whether we like it or not, in a different category to those who have never smoked. We know what it was like, and sometimes, usually under difficult circumstances, we may forget all that we've learned and all the positive training techniques set out in this book.

If you do start to smoke once more, *don't worry*. Don't feel ashamed or guilty or feel that everything to do with giving up was too difficult for you. It wasn't, and you know it. Most people who give up have already given up at least once without success. I know. I did. If you start smoking again and want to give up once more, this time start to read from the beginning of chapter 2 (p. 17) and once more work your way on through this book.

Always remember what was said in the introduction and chapter 4: YOU CAN DO IT IF YOU REALLY WANT TO, BUT YOU HAVE TO REALLY WANT TO BEFORE YOU CAN DO IT. If you really want to, you can and will do it, but you have to accept with a single mind that you *are* going to quit.

Your example in giving up will encourage others to make the attempt. As more adults stop smoking fewer children will start.

Always remember to look ahead. Never look back and regret what you have done. Life is so much better without the 'weed', the 'coughin' nails' or 'cancer sticks'. You are so much healthier and stronger, both physically and mentally. You have so much more time to do things; you have more money to spend; you live a safer life; above all, you are free.

You now know the true and sad results of smoking tobacco. You have chosen and are now in charge. You can do whatever you want to do. Go forward, and be happy.

Useful Addresses

When writing for information please enclose a stamped addressed envelope. All addresses and telephone numbers are correct at the time of going to press.

Action on Smoking and Health (ASH)
National Office
109 Gloucester Place
London W1H 3PH
071 935 3519

National Society of Non Smokers (QUIT)
102 Gloucester Place
London W1H 3DA
071 487 2858

Scottish ASH
Royal College of Physicians
8 Frederick Street
Edinburgh EH2 2HB
031 225 4725

British Acupuncture Accreditation Board
179 Gloucester Place
London NW1 6DX
071 724 5330

British Heart Foundation
Head Office
14 Fitzhardinge Street
London W1H 4DH
071 935 0185

British Medical Association (BMA)
BMA House
Tavistock Square
London WC1V 9JP
071 387 4499

Cancer Research Campaign
Headquarters & London Regional Office
Cambridge House
6 Cambridge Terrace
London NW1 4JL
071 224 1333

Chest Heart and Stroke Association
CHSA House
123–127 Whitecross Street
London EC1Y 8JJ
071 490 7999

Coronary Prevention Group (CPG)
102 Gloucester Place
London W1H 3DA
071 935 2889

Health Education Authority
Hamilton House
Mabledon Place
London WC1H 9TX
071 383 3833

Imperial Cancer Research Fund
Head Office
Labs & Offices
44 Lincolns Inn Fields
London WC2
071 242 0200

QUIT – See National Society of Non Smokers (p. 117)

Women's Therapy Centre
6 Manor Gardens
London N7 6LA
071 263 6200

SMOKESTOP
Department of Psychology
University of Southampton
Southampton S09 5NH
0703 583741

STOP SMOKING!
PO Box 100
Plymouth PL1 1RG
0752 709506

The Teachers' Advisory Council for Alcohol and Drug Education (TACADE)
1 Hulme Place
The Crescent
Salford M5 4QA
061 745 8925

Women's Therapy Centre
6 Manor Gardens
London N7 6LA
071 263 6200